making metal
Jewelry

making metal Jewelry

Projects

Techniques

Inspiration

Joanna Gollberg

LARK BOOKS
A Division of Sterling Publishing Co., Inc.
New York

Editor: **Marthe Le Van**
Art Director: **Kathleen Holmes**
Cover Designer: **Barbara Zaretsky**
Assistant Editor: **Heather Smith**
Production Assistance: **Shannon Yokeley**
Editorial Assistance: **Delores Gosnell**
Photographer: **keithwright.com**
Illustrator: **Orrin Lundgren**

Library of Congress Cataloging-in-Publication Data
Gollberg, Joanna L.
    Making metal jewelry : projects, techniques, inspiration /
        Joanna L. Gollberg.
    p. cm.
    Includes index.
    ISBN 1-57990-347-9 (hard)
    1. Jewelry making.   2. Metal-work.   I. Title.
TT212 .G65 2002
739.27—dc21
                        2002028643

10 9 8 7 6 5 4 3

Published by Lark Books, a division of
Sterling Publishing Co., Inc.
387 Park Avenue South, New York, N.Y. 10016

© 2003, Joanna Gollberg

Distributed in Canada by Sterling Publishing,
c/o Canadian Manda Group, One Atlantic Ave., Suite 105
Toronto, Ontario, Canada M6K 3E7

Distributed in the U.K. by: Guild of Master Craftsman
Publications Ltd. Castle Place, 166 High Street, Lewes, East
Sussex, England BN7 1XU Tel: (+ 44) 1273 477374,
Fax: (+ 44) 1273 478606, E-mail: pubs@thegmcgroup.com,
Web: www.gmcpublications.com

Distributed in Australia by Capricorn Link (Australia) Pty Ltd.,
P.O. Box 704, Windsor, NSW 2756 Australia

If you have questions or comments about this book,
please contact:
Lark Books
67 Broadway
Asheville, NC 28801
(828) 253-0467

Manufactured in China

ISBN 1-57990-347-9

Contents

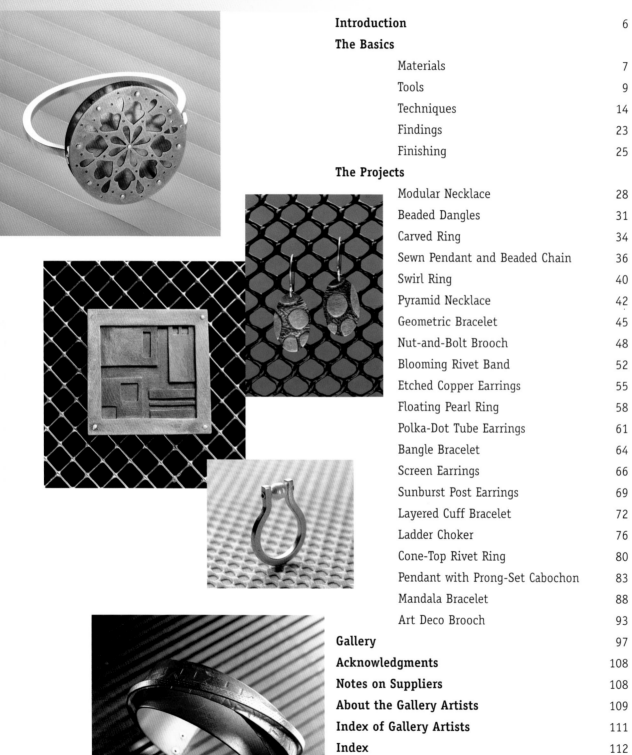

Introduction

COLD-CONNECTING METAL IS the ideal starting place for beginning jewelry makers. Without having to solder or use a torch, you can create high-quality pieces you'll be proud to wear. Once you learn some simple ways to join metal, you'll be able to fashion a wide array of attractive jewelry, using tools that are inexpensive and readily available. The techniques you'll discover provide a solid base for all types of metal work.

For experienced jewelery makers, cold connecting offers a new world of incredibly imaginative design possibilities. It's a dynamic field that is always growing, with more and more jewelers achieving beautiful and inventive results.

In the first chapter of the book, The Basics, you'll be introduced to the materials, tools, and techniques for making cold-connected jewelry—piercing and sawing, riveting, chasing, making jump rings, and finishing. As you take your first steps as a jeweler, remember that you have nothing to lose, only knowledge to gain.

Once you're experienced with the basics, it's time to make your own amazing jewelry. The second section of the book, The Projects, consists of more than 20 designs for earrings, necklaces, bracelets, rings, pendants, and brooches. Feel free to make my pieces exactly as shown, or alter my designs by using different types of metal, adding a texture or patina, replacing a stone with a found object—the variations are endless. I hope you'll use my projects as a springboard to create jewelry that reflects your personal vision of the world, your sense of design, and commitment to quality.

As with design, you also can experiment with materials. This book focuses on metal, but the techniques lend themselves for use with all kinds of jewelry components. You can rivet anything together, such as a piece of colored plastic laminate and pierced metal. You can pierce and saw almost anything. Try using your new jewelry skills on plastic, wood, found objects, and other natural materials. This is a great place to show off your creativity. Look for materials that you think are beautiful, and combine them with metal to make jewelry you'll be pleased both to have designed and to wear. Recently, at an artists' conference, the speaker reminded us to be playful in our work—that through playfulness comes a rich product; that through playfulness the soul of a person will show in his or her work.

In an extensive gallery of contemporary jewelry, you'll see incredible cold-connected pieces made from tin cans and road signs, as well as from sterling silver and gold. These images were included to delight and inspire you. I urge you also to visit jewelry galleries, craft fairs, and supply stores, and talk to other people who make jewelry. Keeping your eyes, ears, and mind open helps you to determine what styles and techniques *you* like; it can influence and encourage your original designs.

When I was in grade school, the teachers gave out awards called "The Extra Mile." The quote that exemplified this award was: "Be the labor great or small, do it well or not at all." Anyone can make jewelry, but those who want to make *good* jewelry will go "the extra mile" and make their jewelry *well*. Whether you're taking it up as a hobby or you want to make your living from making jewelry, do it well. Take time to practice. If you're frustrated and feel you've failed, repeat the technique or step if need be. For me, this is the hardest part of being a jeweler, and I constantly must remind myself of my motto. I hope you enjoy the process and find great satisfaction with the results.

The Basics

Materials

Metal is a wonderful material. There are many different types of *nonferrous* metals, metals not containing iron, that you can use to create jewelry. We'll mostly be working with brass, copper, sterling silver (92.5% fine silver, 7.5% copper), and fine silver (99.9% silver), but you should experiment with other metals too, such as iron, stainless steel, niobium, or aluminum. These metals vary in color, and they can be mixed for interesting effects.

There are two distinct ways of working with nonferrous metals. The first is called *cold metal work*, and the second is called *hot metal work*. All of the jewelry projects in this book are cold worked. Hot metal work uses a torch. We won't use a torch or solder at all in this book.

Sheet metals, left to right: brass, copper, sterling silver

E. Douglas Wunder. Brooch, 1998. 1³/4 x 1³/4 x ¹/4 in. (4.4 x 4.4 x .6 cm). Silver, titanium; constructed with cold connections. Photo by Larry Sanders

Sheet metals, left to right: aluminum, nickel

Sheet Metal and Wire

Metal is sold in a variety of forms, such as sheet, wire, tubing, and grain. In this book we'll use sheet, wire, and tubing. Sheet and wire are measured in a standard gauge system known as the American Wire Gauge (AWG) system (previously called the Brown & Sharp, or B & S, system). Gauges inversely indicate the metal's thickness—the higher the gauge number, the thinner the metal. Gauges differ slightly between metal manufacturers, but not enough to affect our projects. Sheet metal is always flat, but you can purchase it in many different shapes, such as round discs. Wire also can be purchased in various forms, such as round, square, half-round, triangular, and bar. Sheet metal and wire are available through metal suppliers and some jewelry supply houses.

Sheet metal in assorted gauges

Metals forms, clockwise from top left: brass wire, silver shaped wires, assorted tubing, gold grain, fine silver grain, nickel wire

Sheet metal in different shapes

Metal wire in assorted shapes and thicknesses

Metal Tubing

Metal tubing is measured in millimeters or fractions of 1 inch (2.5 cm). Tubing's outside diameter, or *OD*, is the diameter of the exterior tube walls. Its inside diameter, or *ID*, is the diameter of the interior tube walls. Metal tubing is sold in many different wall thicknesses. The tubing you'll use most often for these projects has a wall thickness of .3 mm. (I wouldn't recommend using tubing with walls less than .3 mm or greater than .5 mm thick.)

Tools

The tools for cold-metal working are much less expensive than hot-metal working. You can buy all of these tools at most jewelry supply stores. I've included only the tools required to make the projects in this book.

Bench Pin

When sawing metal, you'll place it on top of a bench pin. Bench pins come in many different styles and sizes. If you don't have a jeweler's bench, you'll need a portable bench pin to put on your worktable. Bench pins are sold at jewelry supply stores.

Steel Block

When hammering metal, you'll place it on top of a steel block. Any piece of flat, smooth, polished steel will work as a steel block, or you can buy a classic jeweler's steel block from any jewelry supply house.

Stainless Steel Ruler

A stainless steel ruler should have a straight edge that isn't nicked or chipped. It should indicate both inches and millimeters. Metric measurements are standard in jewelry making and will be used throughout this book. Fortunately, it's easier and more precise to count in millimeters.

Separators

You'll use separators to measure equal distances. You can purchase separators at stores that cater to tool-and-die makers, machine shops, and the jewelry industry.

Digital Calipers

Digital calipers take precise measurements. I like digital calipers more than analog calipers because the readout is exact. Calipers are great for measuring wire diameters and sheet metal thicknesses. You also can lock digital calipers at a certain measurement, and then use them as a scribe.

Clockwise from top right: bench pin, steel block, wooden dapping block, small steel block

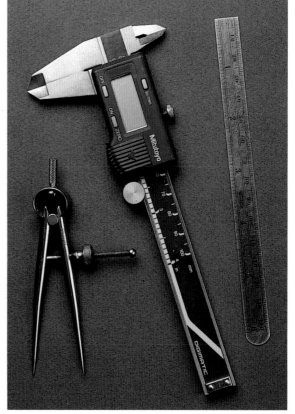

Left to right: separators, digital calipers, steel ruler

Templates

Templates are plastic sheets with precut and sized holes for tracing. I keep a variety of square-, circle-, and oval-shaped templates on hand. They're great for designing and tracing precise shapes onto metal with a scribe. I prefer metric-based templates, but you can also use templates based on the U.S. measurement system. If you don't know your ring size, you can find it easily by first inserting your finger in a circle template, and then placing the correct hole onto a ring mandrel. (The ring mandrel is marked with sizes.)

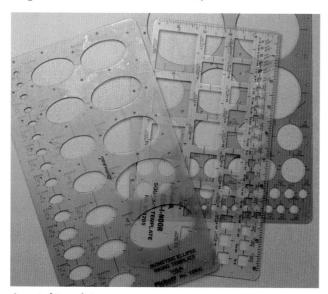

Assorted templates

Geoffrey Giles. *Rounding, Square, Circle, Triangle,* 2001. 1$\frac{1}{8}$ x 1$\frac{1}{8}$ x $\frac{5}{8}$ in. (2.8 x 2.8 x .6 cm). Sterling silver, 14K yellow gold; cold connected. Photo by Taylor Dabney

Scribe

A scribe is a pointed metal "pencil" you use to mark on metal. You can purchase a commercial scribe or make your own by filing the end of a hanger or nail to a sharp point.

Center Punch

This can be any kind of tool with a point on one end and a flat surface to hammer on the other.

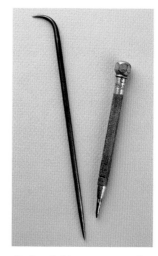

Scribe (left), center punch (right)

You'll use a center punch for making *dimples*, the small indentations made on metal prior to drilling. Dimples also can be decorative marks.

Chasing Hammer

This is a *ball-peen hammer*, a hammerhead with one end shaped like a ball and the other end like a regular flat-faced hammer. A chasing hammer is smaller than a regular hammer and is specially weighted for jewelry making.

Bottom to top: wooden mallet, chasing hammer, rawhide mallet

Wooden or Rawhide Mallet

These large flat-faced hammers are good for forming metal without distorting the metal surface.

Flexible-Shaft Machine

The flexible-shaft machine is an extremely convenient jewelry tool that functions somewhat like a rotary drill. Like a sewing machine, a flexible shaft is motorized with different speeds controlled by a foot pedal. It has a longer, more flexible shaft and a smaller chuck than a regular drill, which is necessary for inserting small accessories such as drill bits.

Drill Bits and Other Flexible-Shaft Machine Accessories

There are countless flexible-shaft accessories on the market. We'll use the flexible shaft primarily for drilling and sanding, but you can have a larger selection of accessories on hand if you wish.

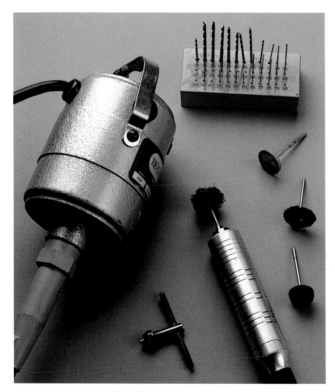

Clockwise from left: flexible-shaft machine, assorted drill bits on wood block, assorted finishing accessories, chuck key

Saw Frame and Saw Blades

A jeweler's saw frame is one of the most important tools in jewelry making. There are many different types of saw frames available, but to accomplish the projects in this book, you'll only need a basic saw frame with a standard 80 mm throat. There also are many different sizes and types of saw blades available. I suggest using size 1/0, 2/0, or 3/0 saw blades (the 3/0 blades are smaller than the 1/0 blades). Go ahead and invest in good quality blades; poor quality blades, though less expensive, often break.

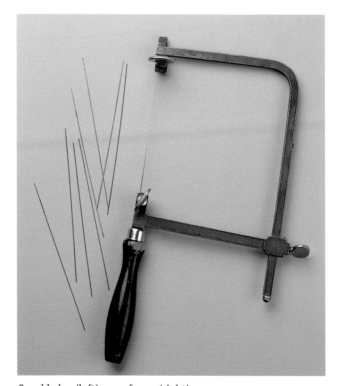

Saw blades (left), saw frame (right)

Snips

At first glance, snips resemble pliers. Snips have tapered ends with two cutting blades that come together to cut wire up to 16 gauge. Many types of snips are sold at hardware stores, craft shops, or jewelry supply houses. Extra large nail clippers also make great snips.

Needle Files

These files are perfect to use on small metal jewelry parts. Needle files allow you to file in hard-to-reach places. We'll use the round, half-round, square, triangular, and barrette needle files. These files look exactly as their names suggest, except the barrette file, which is flat on one side with no teeth on the other triangular side. Files only remove metal on the forward stroke; the metal is simply scratched on the backward stroke, not removed.

Bastard File

This is a large file you can buy for a reasonable price at any hardware store. It should be fairly coarse, but you should still be able to run your fingers along the file without catching your skin on its teeth.

Left to right: round needle file, half-round needle file, bastard needle file, barrette needle file, triangular needle file, square needle file, half-round needle file

Pliers (Flat Nose, Chain Nose, Round Nose)

These pliers are shaped much as their names suggest. The flat-nose pliers have two flat sides that meet on the inside and at a flat angle on the outside of the noses. Chain-nose pliers are flat on the inside, round on the outside, and tapered almost to a point. Round-nose pliers are round inside and out and taper to a point.

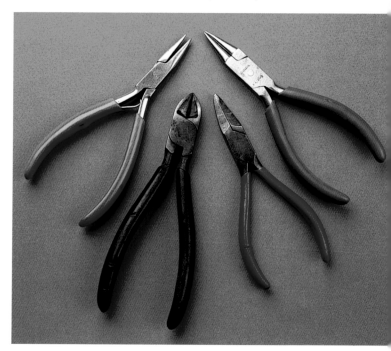

Left to right: chain-nose pliers, snips, flat-nose pliers, round-nose pliers

Flaring Tool

This can be any small hand tool that is tapered at one end and flat at the other. I use an old burr, which once was an attachment for my flexible shaft. It's broken off at the end, nicely tapered, and perfect for beginning to open, or *flare*, a piece of tubing for riveting. You also can use a chasing tool that is tapered almost to a point.

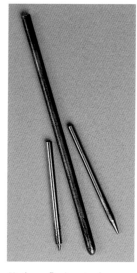

Various flaring tools

Mandrels

A mandrel is any form that you can wrap metal around. Some mandrels are tapered, such as ring and bracelet mandrels, while others are the same diameter for their whole length. You can use anything as a mandrel, even ordinary items you find around your house, such as a dowel or pencil. Ring and bracelet mandrels are available only through jewelry supply houses.

Left to right: oval bracelet mandrel, tube mandrel, wire mandrel, round bracelet mandrel, three small mandrels, ring mandrel, large tube mandrel

Chasing Tools

Chasing marks are one way to texturize or pattern the surface of metal. Chasing tools make the impressions on the metal. These steel tools can be round or square and have an endless variety of shapes carved into the end.

Assorted chasing tools

Sandpaper

The type of sandpaper that works best on metal is called *wet/dry sandpaper*. (The grit on regular sandpaper isn't affixed well enough to use with metal.) It's helpful to remember that the higher the number, the finer the grit. Jewelers most often use 220- and 400-grit paper.

Clockwise from right: 400-grit sandpaper, fine-grit steel wool, coarse-grit steel wool, green kitchen scrub

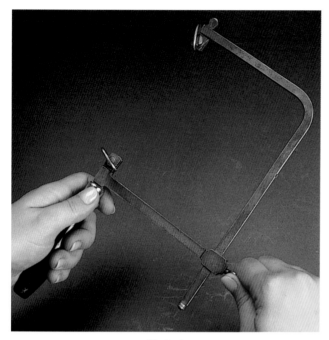

Photo 1

Photo 2

Techniques

There are several metal jewelry techniques you'll use over and over as you create the projects in this book. These are the fundamentals of cold working. To learn these basic procedures, I suggest practicing the following techniques until you are comfortable with your new skills.

Piercing and Sawing

Piercing and sawing is the first technique you'll need to know in order to create cold-connected jewelry.

Installing a Saw Blade into a Saw Frame

Open the jaw of the saw frame to a length approximately 10 mm shorter than the length of the saw blade (see photo 1). Insert the saw blade into the top nut of the frame, with the teeth facing toward you and pointing down. Tighten the nut. Rest the end of the saw frame handle on your sternum, and rest the top edge of the saw frame against the side of your worktable or jeweler's bench. Push the saw handle in with your sternum to slightly shorten the length of the jaw (see photo 2). With the jaw length shortened, place the end of the blade into the lower nut, and tighten (see photo 3). Release the pressure on the handle. Your saw blade should be quite taut in the frame.

Before You Begin to Saw

It's helpful to saw near your eye level. This arrangement makes it easier to see what you're doing, and saves you

Photo 3

from unnecessary backaches. Either have a short stool for sawing at a table of normal height or work at a table higher than normal. My jeweler's bench is about 1 foot (30.5 cm) taller than most regular tables for this purpose.

Sawing Tips

Always hold the saw lightly in your hand and let the saw teeth do all the work on the downward stroke. Use your hand simply as a guide for sawing, not for exerting pressure. Beginning jewelers usually break a lot of saw blades. No need to fret if this happens to you—you'll become quite proficient with a little practice.

Sawing Metal

Place the metal on the bench pin. Move the saw frame up and down, always keeping it at a 90° angle to the metal (see photo 4). Keep the frame pointing forward at all times, unless you're turning a sharp corner. Turn the metal for rounding a corner or sawing an arc, not the saw frame. To turn a sharp corner, simultaneously turn the saw and the metal while quickly moving the saw up and down.

Photo 4

Piercing Metal

To pierce a piece of sheet metal, you'll need a center punch, a hammer, a flexible shaft, and an assortment of drill bits. I recommend purchasing a drill-bit assortment from a jewelry supply house, as the bits are sized specifically for jewelry making. The drill bits you buy at hardware stores work for some techniques, but they are usually too large for our projects.

1. Decide where you want to drill a hole. While resting the metal on the steel block, lightly use the center punch and hammer to make a *dimple*, or small indentation on the metal as shown in photo 5. This mark guides the drill bit. If you don't indent the metal surface, the drill bit will swerve over the sheet metal, making extra marks that will have to be sanded off later. Furthermore, the hole may not be drilled exactly where you want it.

Photo 5

2. Securely insert the drill bit into the flexible shaft. Drill the hole on top of a wooden surface as shown in photo 6 (I keep a scrap wood piece specifically for drilling).

Photo 6

3. Thread the saw blade through the drilled hole as shown in photo 7, attach it to the bottom nut on the saw frame, and tighten the frame. Saw as described on pages 14 and 15, creating cutout or *negative* spaces inside the framework of the metal.

Photo 7

Steve Midgett. *Love Letters Brooch*, 1995. 2¼ x 1½ in. (5.7 x 3.8 cm). Sterling silver, brass, copper; cold connected. Photo by artist

Riveting

A rivet securely traps pieces of metal together. A rivet literally passes through layers of metal, and then is flared on each side to hold the material. There are two types of rivets: tube rivets and wire rivets. Both types function the same, but look different, and both can be wonderful decorative accents. "Practice makes perfect" is the best motto for learning to rivet.

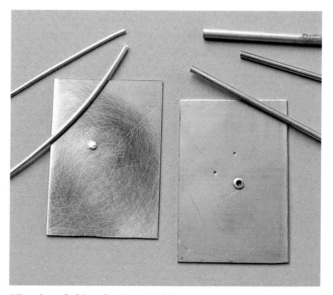

Wire rivet (left), tube rivet (right)

Wire Riveting

1. Use the caliper to measure the thickness of the metals you want to connect (see photo 8).

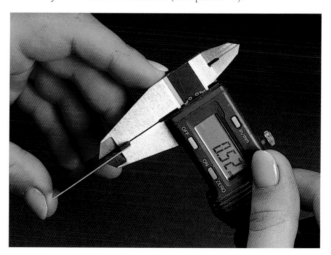

Photo 8

2. Dimple the metal, and then drill a hole through each layer you want to join as shown in photo 9. Make the hole the same diameter as the round wire you plan to use for the rivets.

3. Use the saw to cut a length of wire about 2 mm longer than the thickness of the metal layers (see photo 10). Sand the ends of the cut wire with 400-grit paper. Thread the wire through the holes drilled in the metal as shown in photo 11.

4. Place the threaded metal on top of the steel block. Use the chasing hammer to gently tap the end of the wire two or three times as shown in photo 12, and then turn the metal piece over. Adjust the length of the wire so there is an equal amount poking out of each side of the hole. Make two or three gentle taps on the reverse side, and turn the piece over again. Repeat this process until the wire ends "mushroom" (see photo 13), forming the rivet and securing the metal layers.

Photo 9

Photo 10

Photo 11

Photo 12

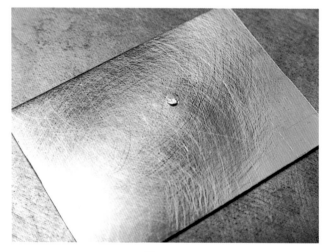

Photo 13

TROUBLESHOOTING If the wire bends before the rivet is complete, you may have cut the rivet wire too long. The other possibility is that you didn't turn over the metal enough times to rivet the wire ends in equal amounts. In wire riveting it's essential to keep turning the piece over and mushrooming the wire ends equally. You absolutely cannot completely mushroom one end, and then turn the piece over and mushroom the other end.

HINT Practice riveting by drilling a hole through only one layer of metal. Use a large 14- or 16-gauge wire for ease and clarity during the learning process. With the saw frame and blade, saw the wire into lengths. Don't cut the wire with the snips since they leave an uneven end on the wire. Practice riveting several times with the thicker wire, and then practice with smaller gauges. (To make strong rivets, however, never use any wire thinner than 20 gauge.) By practicing in this manner, you'll quickly gain control of your wire rivets.

Harriete Estel Berman. Beads, 2001. 1/8–1/4 in. (3.5–7 mm) diameter. Preprinted steel, thermoplastic, colored electrical wire, polymer clay, sterling silver; formed with hydraulic press, connected with oversized tube rivets. Photo by Philip Cohen

Tube Riveting

1. Measure the thickness of the metals you want to connect (see photo 8, page 16).

2. Dimple the metal, and then drill a hole through each layer you want to join (see photo 9, page 17). Make the hole the same diameter as the tubing you plan to use for the rivets.

3. Use the saw to cut a length of tubing about 2 mm longer than the thickness of the metal layers (see photo 14). Sand the ends of the cut tubing with 400-grit paper. Thread the tubing through the holes drilled in the metal as shown in photo 15.

Photo 14

Photo 15

4. Place the threaded metal piece on top of the steel block. Insert the flaring tool into the end of the tubing (see photo 16). Using the chasing hammer, make one light tap on the flaring tool. Turn the metal piece over, insert the flaring tool into the end of the tubing, and make one light tap.

5. With the flaring tool and chasing hammer, continue making one tap at a time on each end of the tubing until the tubing cannot be removed from the drilled hole (see photo 17).

6. Continue to flare the tubing without using the flaring tool. Make gentle taps directly on the tubing with the ball side of the chasing hammer. Make sure to continually turn the piece over and tap an equal amount on both sides. Tap the tubing until the rivet is secure as shown in photo 18.

Photo 16

TROUBLESHOOTING If the tube rivet isn't evenly flared, you may have cut the tubing too long, or you may not have flared the tubing properly (step 4). If the tube rivet splits open, you either hammered too much, too fast, or hammered with too much force. If the flared tubing is different lengths, you didn't equalize the length of the tubing each time you turned the piece over.

HINT Practice making tube rivets just as you practiced making wire rivets. In this case, however, start with tubing about 3 to 4 mm OD. Make several practice rivets with tubing this size, and then practice some more with larger and smaller tubing. This gives you an excellent idea of how tubing responds to the flaring tool and the chasing hammer.

Photo 17

Photo 18

Chasing

Chasing allows you to make imprints into sheet metal without removing any metal. The process uses chasing tools, a hammer, and a steel block. You can design a piece of jewelry with chasing as the central focus, or you can add a bit of chasing here and there for extra interest or texture. While I have only used chasing on some of the projects in this book, feel free to always consider it as a design option and apply the technique wherever you wish.

Chased design element

Chasing Tools

Most jewelry supply houses sell commercial chasing tools. You also can make your own tools by filing pieces of scrap steel, such as old screwdrivers. I have a matting tool that is actually an old flat-head screwdriver marred on one end. (A *matting tool* is a chasing tool that makes a more complex texture design or imprint on the metal.) For a long-lasting, handmade chasing tool, you can order tool steel, file it into a specific design on one end, and then harden and temper the steel. These handmade tools are fun to make and satisfying to use. A wide variety of commercial stamps also are available. Sometimes these stamps are made carelessly and their designs uneven, but you can use needle files to reshape the stamp into its proper design. Keep your eye out at flea markets and junk shops for chasing tools—they often appear in unexpected places.

Commercial stamps

Chasing and Stamping Metal

With the metal taped to the steel block, hold the chasing tool in your fingers, and lightly tap it on the metal with the chasing hammer as shown in photo 19. Experiment by making light and hard hammer taps to see the different impressions you can make. Because it gives resistance to the hammer blows, the steel block is essential to this process. Otherwise, the metal may become deformed, and the stamp or chasing tool can't properly do its job. When using commercial stamps, I find that one hammer blow is never sufficient to imprint the metal. I use firm taps with the chasing hammer, and vertically rock the stamp back and forth to make sure I imprint the whole design (see photo 20).

After chasing, the metal may become slightly domed. To flatten the metal, turn it over on the steel block so the chasing faces down and lightly hammer the surface with a wooden hammer or a rawhide mallet. This type of hammer is great for moving and shaping metal without leaving unwanted imprints on the surface. You may need to repeat this process several times during one chasing session.

Photo 19

Photo 20

Laying Out a Design

Figures 1 and 2 are two templates for determining measurements. The circle divider template (figure 1) is extremely useful for marking even spaces around a circle. Simply lay a metal circle or ring on top of the same-size circle template, and mark the metal with the scribe. You'll refer to this template for projects such as Sunburst Post Earrings (page 69) and Cone-Top Rivet Ring (page 80). I've found it very useful to photocopy and laminate these templates. This way they're durable and accessible.

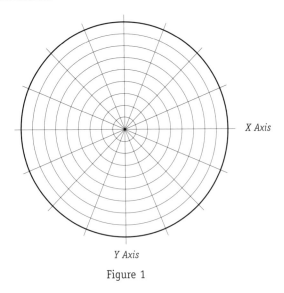

X Axis

Y Axis

Figure 1

Figure 2 calculates the length of metal you'll need to make a particular ring size. For 24-gauge metal, this is the exact measurement you'll need to cut for a metal band ring. To use a thicker metal, add one and one-half times the thickness of the metal to the required length to determine size. Once you know your ring size, use the steel ruler to measure from the end line to the line marking for the size. You'll refer to this chart for projects such as Swirl Ring (page 40) and Blooming Rivet Band (page 52).

0 1 2 3 4 5 6 7 8 9 10 11 12 13

Figure 2

Transferring a Design onto Metal

Once you design a piece of jewelry on paper, you'll have to transfer the design onto metal. When transferring any design onto metal, conserve as much surface space as possible to conserve metal. Don't start a design in the center of a metal sheet; instead, place the design near the edge or corner. Often, you can use the straight lines of the metal edges to save yourself some sawing.

Since most of my projects are based on geometric forms, they can be easily and directly drawn onto metal with a scribe and the plastic design templates, the steel ruler, or the separators. However, if your jewelry design is more organic in form, you'll need to transfer your design in another way. Here are several options.

Carbon Paper

Draw a design on paper or photocopy a pattern. Insert a piece of carbon paper between the design and the sheet metal. Use tape to secure both the paper and the carbon paper to the metal. Trace the design with a pencil as shown in photo 21. Once the carbon copy is on the metal, trace back over the whole design with the scribe so the design won't smudge off (see photo 22).

Photo 21   Photo 22

Stipple Marks

Draw a design on paper or photocopy a pattern. Place the paper on top of the sheet metal. Tape the paper to the metal so it doesn't move. Use the tip of the scribe or a sharp needle to make *stipple marks*, or tiny pricks, along the lines of the design and into the metal as shown in photo 23.

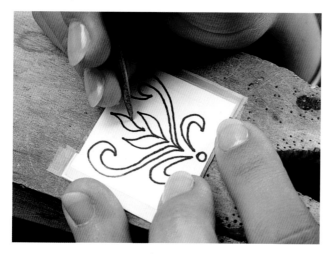

Photo 23

Chinese White

Chinese White is a white, slightly waxy substance that comes in a small 1-inch (2.5 cm) block, often wrapped in aluminum foil. You can buy Chinese White at jewelry supply or art supply stores that carry paint products. Using Chinese White to transfer jewelry designs is a traditional technique.

Photo 24

Draw a design on paper or photocopy a pattern. Use a soft-lead pencil to completely "black out" the back side of the drawing as shown in photo 24. Wet your finger with some saliva, rub the block of Chinese White, and then paint the Chinese White onto the metal (see photo 25). Make a nice even layer of white on the metal as shown in photo 26, and let dry. Tape the drawing to the metal with the design facing up, and trace the design with a pencil. After transferring the drawing, trace back over the lines with a scribe so the design doesn't smudge.

Photo 25

Photo 26

Findings

The term *findings* means jewelry parts, such as earwires, clasps, bales, ear posts, and ear nuts. You can buy commercial findings or make your own. Handmade findings, if secure and well constructed, are much nicer than commercial findings. I use commercial earring posts and nuts in my work, but make all other findings by hand. I strongly believe that jewelry findings should be made of metal comparable to the actual piece of jewelry. For example, if I were making a sterling silver pendant, I would never use a base metal chain. If my earrings are sterling silver, I want my earwires to be sterling as well. For some projects, I've recommended the use of commercial findings so you can concentrate on creating the main jewelry piece. Once you've mastered the basic cold-connection techniques, I urge you to make your own findings when possible. An interesting handmade finding really completes an original design and makes it wholly special.

Clasps (left and top), bales (right)

Left to right: ear posts, ear wires, ear nuts

Jump Rings

Jump rings are made from wire and used for connecting elements in a piece of jewelry. The rings have a sawed slit, which means you can open and close the circles. You can easily make all types of jump rings from any gauge wire, although very thick wire may be hard to manipulate.

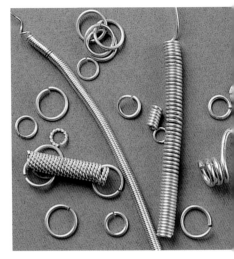

Assorted jump rings

To make jump rings, you'll need a selection of mandrels. I use tubing, the ends of files, the ends of drill bits, and any plain wire stock I have on hand.

Making Jump Rings

1. Cut a length of wire, and tightly wrap it around a mandrel as shown in photo 27. Each complete wrap makes one jump ring. Once you have made the number of wraps needed (see photo 28), slide the wire coil off the mandrel. If the coil is longer than 1 or 1½ inches (2.5 or 3.8 cm), you may want to trim it down. A shorter coil is easier to hold and saw.

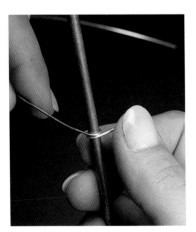

Photo 27

Photo 28

2. Tightly holding the coil in your fingers, place it on top of the bench pin. Saw down the length of the coil, holding the saw at a slight angle as shown in photo 29. Be very careful when sawing apart jump rings—it's easy for the saw to slip and cut your fingers. (Have some flexible plastic bandages near your work station at all times just in case.)

Photo 29

Opening and Closing Jump Rings

Now that you have a nice pile of open jump rings, you'll need to know how to properly open and close them. Hold one side of the open ring in the flat-nose pliers, and hold the other side in the chain-nose pliers (see photo 30). Move the ends from side to side, not open and closed like a lobster claw—this is the essential part of opening and closing jump rings. Only open a jump ring as much as needed to insert the metal you're joining. If you open the ring too wide, the shape can become distorted. To make a simple chain, join jump rings together, one after another (see photo 31).

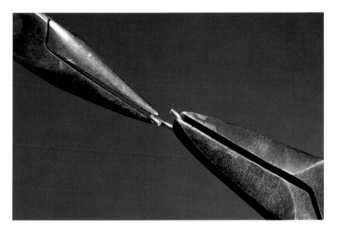

Photo 30

Photo 31

Finishing

Finishing is an integral part of metal work. The finish of the piece can enhance and complete a jewelry design. There is a wide variety of finishing options. A piece can be matte, shiny, or have a *patina*, a coloration or blackening of the metal.

Sanding

There are many options for sanding metal. Hand sanding is the most labor-intensive. It also takes much longer than using a sanding attachment on the flexible shaft. Sanding discs snap onto a mandrel. Split mandrels also are made for the flexible shaft. Here, you insert a strip of sandpaper and wrap it around the mandrel. (This is my preferred method.) There are also new plastic bristle discs. I find the bristle discs work better for finishing than they do for actually removing metal. Experiment with these sanding options to find which one works best for you.

When sanding a piece of jewelry, I usually start with the 220-grit sandpaper. This removes most scribe lines and deeper marks. Next, I use the 400-grit paper to completely sand over my first pass. It's a good practice

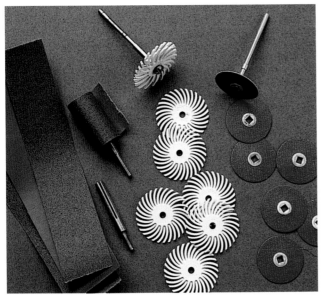

Left to right: split mandrels with sand papers, plastic bristle discs, sanding discs

to sand with 220-grit in one direction as shown in photo 32, and then sand over that area with 400-grit in the opposite direction (see photo 33). This way you'll know when you've thoroughly sanded your piece with the finer grit. These are the only two sandpaper grits I ever use in my work. Some people suggest sanding with a 600-grit paper before completely finishing, but I find this additional step unnecessary. The choice is yours once you've experimented both ways.

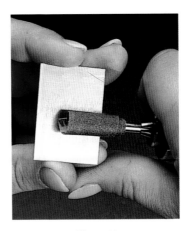

Photo 32   Photo 33

Matte Finish

To create a matte finish, I use 400-grit wet/dry sandpaper, steel wool of various grits, or a green kitchen scrub. You can use any of these tools to make a matte finish. Simply rub one back and forth or in a circular motion on the surface of the metal as shown in photo 34.

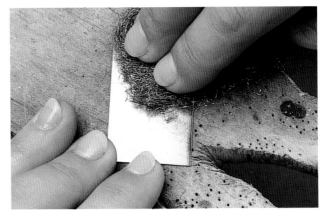

Photo 34

Shiny Finish

For a shiny finish, I use steel-brush attachments in the flexible shaft, a polishing cloth, or a tumbler filled with steel shot. If you don't have a tumbler, the other options work great.

Left to right: polishing cloth, steel brush accessories for flexible shaft, tumbler with steel shot

Patinas

To create a colored metal finish, you can use selenium toner, liver of sulphur, or a blackening agent. Selenium toner is sold at photography stores, while liver of sul-

Left to right: liver of sulphur, black patina, selenium toner

phur and blackening agents are available through jewelry supply houses. Always read and follow the manufacturer's recommendations when working with chemical patinas.

Liver of Sulphur Patina

You can blacken brass or copper by dropping it into a liver of sulphur solution. This simple procedure adds both depth and color to your jewelry. If you've created a surface design, the patina makes it more visible. Liver of sulphur has a strong odor, so I recommend you use it outside or in a well-ventilated area.

In a glass bowl, dissolve one chunk of liver of sulphur in hot water. Drop the piece of jewelry into the solution. Leave the metal in the solution until it turns black, approximately 1 to 2 minutes. (If you leave the piece in the liver of sulphur too long, the black color becomes a thick crust that flakes off later.) Remove the piece from the liver of sulphur solution, and wash it in hot water. The hot water helps the patina adhere to the metal. You may need to repeat this process for a blacker tone. You then can leave the piece black, or rub it with an abrasive such as steel wool, a coarse cleanser, or a green kitchen scrub. This extra rubbing gives the metal a nice final finish that lets the natural metal color show through.

Black Patina

To quickly and easily create a black patina, you can use selenium toner or a chemical blackening agent. Simply drop the piece of jewelry into the chemical solution, wait about 15 seconds, remove with copper tongs or a piece of wire, and then wash in warm water. You may need to repeat this process for a blacker patina. You never should touch these chemicals with your hands. Always wear rubber gloves and work in a well-ventilated area.

The Projects

Now you can put your new skills to work and create a spectacular collection of rings, brooches, necklaces, bracelets, earrings, and pendants—all with cold connections. Each project uses the basic techniques in different combinations to achieve unique results. I've included a wide range of jewelry designs, from pure whimsy to sophisticated elegance, so you'll have plenty of styles from which to choose. Enjoy the satisfaction of making your own jewelry and the joy of expressing yourself through metal.

Modular Necklace

This versatile necklace design lets you create your own link shapes, and the possibilities are infinite. The layout is based on 16 equal-sized metal elements joined by jump rings. The clasp is built into the link design so the necklace flows beautifully. Use a single metal, or vary the color if you like.

WHAT YOU NEED

Steel ruler

Scribe

Sheet metal, 24 or 26 gauge

Chasing hammer and punch

Steel block

Saw frame and blades

Flexible shaft

Drill bit, 1.3 to 1.5 mm

Needle files

Flexible-shaft sanding accessories

Sandpaper, 400- and 220-grit

Wire, 16 or 18 gauge

Round mandrel, approximately 5 mm in diameter

Flat-nose pliers

Chain-nose pliers

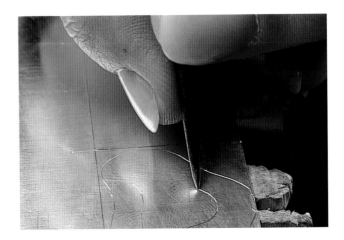

2. Draw a design for each link within each 1-inch (2.5 cm) metal square as shown. Make sure each link design includes space for four holes at the top of the metal where jump rings will attach the links. Pierce and saw out the links.

1. Use the steel ruler and scribe to mark 16 squares on the sheet metal, each 1 x 1 inch (2.5 x 2.5 cm). Draw the squares adjacent to each other to conserve metal (see photo).

3. Dimple, and then drill holes for the jump rings as shown: two holes on each side for four holes on each link. Do not drill one side of one link. This will be used to connect the clasp.

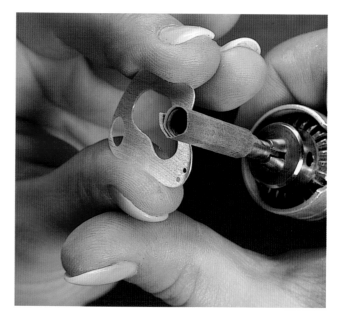

4. Design the handmade clasp. (My clasp looks similar to my links.) Make sure the clasp is long enough to stay connected once it's bent. Pierce and saw out the clasp as shown. Dimple two holes on the clasp for the jump-ring connections, and drill. File if needed, sand the clasp to a 400-grit finish, and give it a final finish if desired. Bend the clasp so it's ready to connect to the necklace.

5. On the link without drilled holes on both sides, pierce and saw out an oval shape for threading the clasp (see photo, lower left). Make sure the clasp fits though nicely and hooks securely into this opening. Sand each link to a 400-grit finish as shown above, and then give each link a final finish.

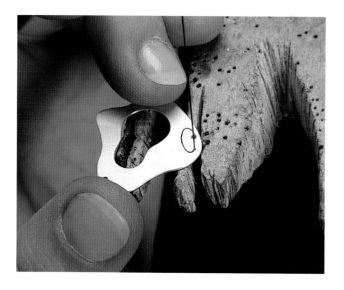

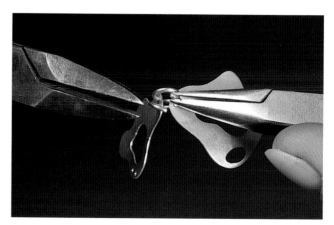

6. Wrap the 16- or 18-gauge wire around a mandrel approximately 5 mm in diameter to make at least 32 jump rings. Make a few extra in case some get lost. Saw apart the jump rings. Use the pliers to join together the links and the clasp with the jump rings (see photo).

Beaded Dangles

These all-purpose earrings are the perfect accessory for both carefree weekends and elegant evenings. A narrow saw line running the length of the earring lightens the appearance of the metal as does the simple French earwire. Use any bead you wish on the dangle. You may want to make several pairs with differently colored beads to complement your outfits.

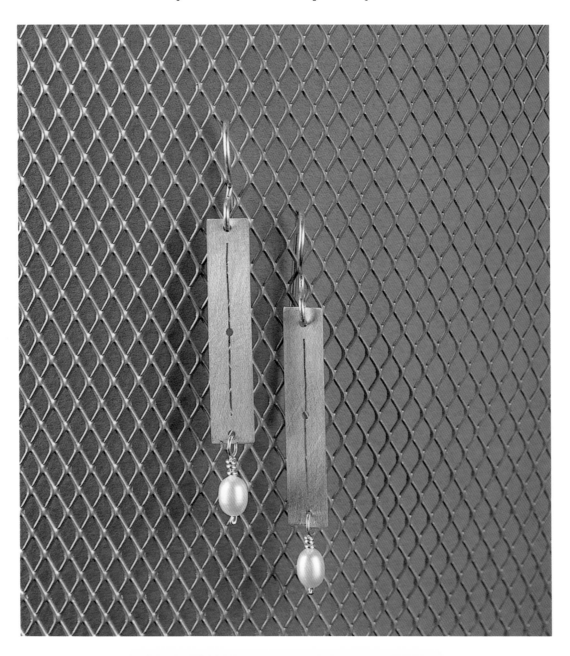

WHAT YOU NEED

Steel ruler

Scribe

Sterling silver sheet metal, 24 gauge

Separators

Saw frame and blades

Needle files

Flexible shaft

Flexible-shaft sanding accessories

Sandpaper, 400- and 220-grit

Medium-grit emery cloth and clipboard (optional)

Chasing hammer and punch

Steel block

Drill bit, 1 mm

Sterling silver wire, 20 gauge

Snips

Round-nose pliers

Chain-nose pliers

2 round mandrels, 10 mm and 2 mm

2 beads for dangles

shown. The board makes a nice flat surface, and its clip holds the emery cloth in place.) Slowly sand back and forth; if you sand too quickly, you can sand off the corners and make them uneven. The same principle applies to filing straight lines.

3. Dimple (see photo) and drill the holes for the French wires, the dangles, and the center saw holes on both rectangles.

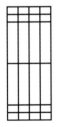

1. Use the steel ruler and scribe to mark two 6 x 30-mm rectangles on the sheet metal. (You can do this in one long line or in two columns as shown. Conserve metal by using one of the sheet's straight edges.) Mark both the vertical and horizontal centerlines on each rectangle. Open the separators to 2 mm (measure this distance on your steel ruler), and mark a line down from the top edge and up from the bottom edge of both rectangles. These marks indicate the hole placements for the earwires and the dangles. Open the separators to 4 mm, and scribe a line on both the top and the bottom of the rectangle. These lines indicate where to stop the decorative saw line.

2. Carefully saw out the rectangles. File or sand the cut edges straight. (I sand straight lines by putting a piece of medium-grit emery cloth on a clipboard as

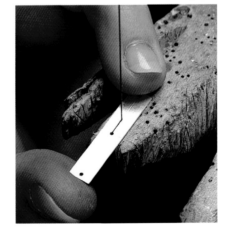

4. Thread the saw blade into one center hole, and carefully saw straight to the stop line as shown. Gently pull the blade back through the saw line, turn the rectangle, and saw to

the other stop line. Unthread the saw blade. Repeat this process on the second rectangle. Sand the rectangles, using a 220-grit and a 400-grit sandpaper. Apply the desired finish to the earrings. (I used a dry green kitchen scrub.)

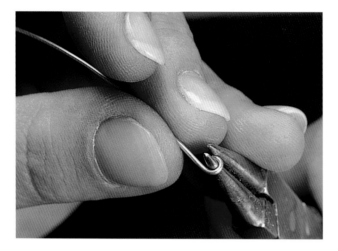

5. For the earwires, snip two pieces of 20-gauge wire, each approximately 45 mm long. Using the round-nose pliers, curve one wire end into a complete circle as shown; then bend the wire at the end of the circle, so the straight wire comes out of the middle of the circle.

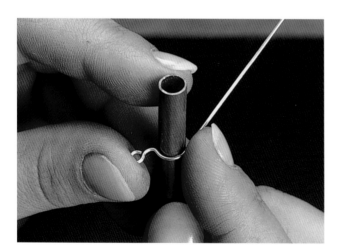

6. With the chain-nose pliers, hold the earwire directly above the circle formed in step 5. Bend the straight wire over the pliers' tips toward you, making sure the opening in the circle faces away from you. Holding the wire with your fingers, bend the rest of

the straight wire around the 10-mm round mandrel to make the part of the earwire that rests in the lobe (see photo, below left). Sand the wire end with 400-grit sandpaper so it doesn't prick your ear. Open the earwire circle with the pliers, thread the rectangle onto the French wire, and close the circle. Repeat steps 5 and 6 to make and install the second earwire.

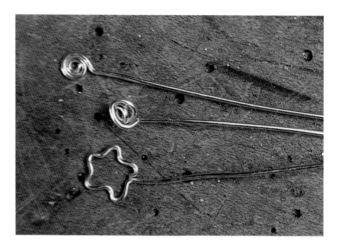

7. To make the dangle wire, bend the end of a 1½-inch (3.8 cm) piece of 20-gauge wire into a tiny U. (As shown in the top right photo, you can make fancier ends 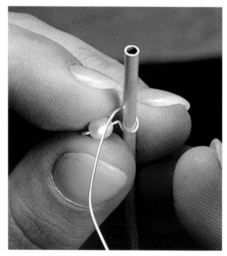 by curling the wire into any shape.) Follow the technique detailed in step 6 to thread the bead of your choice, but instead of holding the wire above the circle, hold it above the bead. Once the wire is bent toward you, wrap the remaining wire around a small mandrel to make a complete circle (see photo, bottom right). Thread the wire through the dangle hole in the rectangle. Wrap the tail around the space left above the bead. Snip off any extra wire.

Carved Ring

Sculpting this band is a great way to practice working
with metal files. The ring is very receptive to different
designs and experimentation. Sterling ring blanks
are fairly inexpensive, so purchase several and
explore the possibilities.

WHAT YOU NEED

Photocopied circle divider template, page 21

Sterling silver square wire ring blank, any size

Scribe

Assorted needle files, such as round, square,
    triangular, and barrette

Flexible shaft

Flexible-shaft sanding accessories

Sandpaper, 400- and 220-grit

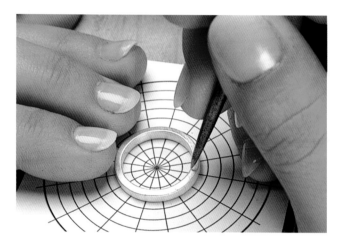

1. Using the photocopied circle divider template, mark the ring with the scribe into sections as shown. (My ring has eight sections.) Start by marking the band on the top of the ring, and then use those marks as guides to mark the sections along the side and the bottom of the ring. Mark the inside of the ring if you wish.

2. File small indentations along each of the scribe lines with the triangular file as shown. Use these as guide marks for your design.

3. File the band in any manner you desire, utilizing the shapes of the needle files. A round needle file makes a U-shape indentation (see photo) and a square needle file can make a triangular-shaped indentation or a square, U-shape indentation. Use the barrette file to shape up and round off corners as you carve. (For an interesting effect, mark the band into eight sections on the top and bottom of the ring, and then file the lines diagonally from point to point instead of vertically.)

4. Sand the carved ring to a 400-grit finish. You might have to do a bit of hand sanding. Fold a piece of sandpaper so you can reach the hard-to-get places (see photo). Finish the ring as desired.

Sewn Pendant and Beaded Chain

Express yourself by making this one-of-a-kind pendant. Cut the sheet metal into any shape you desire, and pierce it as many times as you wish. Sewing with wire is boldly artistic. Adding random beads increases the visual energy of the piece. The pendant becomes more beautiful when strung upon its handmade matching chain.

WHAT YOU NEED

Scribe

Sheet metal, 24 gauge

Saw frame and blades

Needle files

Bastard file

Chasing hammer and punch

Steel block

Flexible shaft

Assorted drill bits

Flexible-shaft sanding accessories

Sandpaper, 400- and 220-grit

Fine silver wire, 24 gauge

Snips

Pearls or beads, more than 40

Chain-nose pliers

Small mandrel, 2 to 3 mm in diameter

Round-nose pliers

Commercial catch and clasp

2. Design the interior of the pendant, using negative shapes within the outer shape. Use large simple interior shapes so the sewing becomes the focal point of the pendant. Include a bale hole in the interior design. Pierce and saw out the interior shapes (see photo). File the cut edges smooth.

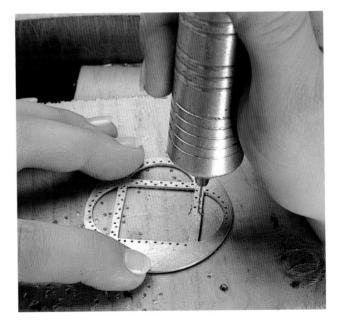

1. Design a shape for the pendant. Scribe the shape onto the sheet metal as shown, and saw out. File the edges of the cut metal.

3. Dimple drill holes about 2 mm outside the edges of the negative shapes. Make as many or as few holes as you wish. The number of holes determines the density of the sewing. (My holes are approximately 2 mm apart.) Drill the holes using a bit slightly larger than the 24-gauge wire (see photo). Drill a slightly larger hole for the bale. Sand the pendant to a 400-grit finish.

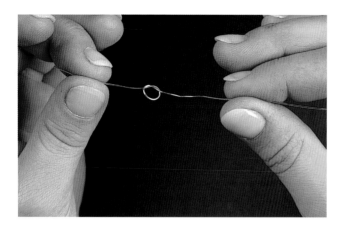

4. Cut a 12-inch (30.5 cm) length of the fine silver wire for sewing. The wire is easier to work with in shorter lengths because it hardens as you sew. Make a simple one-loop knot in the end of the wire as shown. Trim the tail of the knot so it's small and fits snugly next to the metal.

5. Thread the knot through a hole on the back side of the pendant. (The back side will have all the knots.) Feed the wire through random holes, sewing back and forth over the negative shapes as shown. Add a bead or a pearl to the wire at any time for an interesting look. When you run out of sewing wire, simply tie off the end with a knot to secure, or make a tiny bend in the wire to prevent it from coming back through the hole. Begin sewing with a new piece of wire. Repeat this process until the sewing is complete.

6. To make the bale, thread a 6-inch (15.2 cm) piece of wire through the bale hole. Make four or five loops in the wire, each about ⅛ inch (3 mm) in diameter. Wrap the tail of the wire around the loops to hold them together (see photo). Use this wrap as part of the design, or wrap only on the back side of the bale so the wraps remain hidden. Snip off the tail of the wire.

7. To make the 16-inch (40.6 cm) chain, cut approximately 34 pieces of the 24-gauge fine silver wire, each about 3 inches (7.6 cm) long. With the chain-nose pliers, bend each wire into an L shape that has one 2-inch (5 cm) side. Thread a bead or pearl onto the longer side of one L-shaped wire. Using the chain-nose pliers, hold the wire about 2 to 3 mm above the bead. Bend the long wire tail over the bead at a 90° angle (see photo). The bead shouldn't be able to slide off the wire. Repeat this process for all 34 wire pieces.

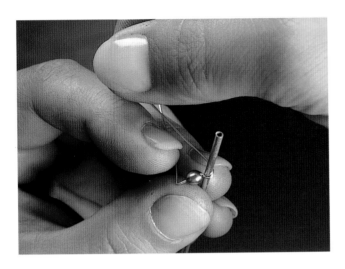

8. To make the loops, completely wrap each tail of the beaded and bent wires around the small mandrel as shown. You can use round-nose pliers, but a mandrel makes more uniform loops. Repeat this process on all 34 pieces.

10. To join the chain links together, thread the open wire tail into a closed wire tail and close the loop (see photo). You should have an equal number of wraps on both sides of the bead in each link. To finish the chain, thread all 34 links together, thread the catch and the clasp, and then close those loops. Thread the sewn pendant onto the chain.

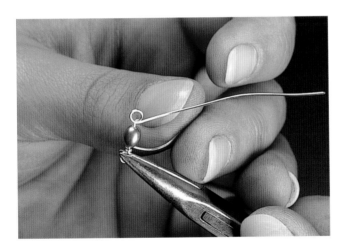

9. Hold one loop in the round-nose pliers to keep the loop in shape. Wrap one wire tail around the space above the bead as shown. Leave room to wrap the other side of the bead. Snip off the wire ends. This process is called *closing the loop*. Close the loop on only one side of 32 pieces; leave 2 pieces completely unclosed for attaching the catch and clasp.

Swirl Ring

Making this beaded wire ring is so quick and easy, you may have one for every finger (and toe?) before you even know it! Experiment with different metal colors, wire gauges, and stones—you'll learn something new with each combination, and since they make great gifts you'll have plenty to share with your friends.

WHAT YOU NEED

  Wire, 12 gauge

  Saw frame and blades or snips

  Flat-nose pliers

  Ring mandrel

  Barrette needle file

  Half-drilled pearl or bead

  Flexible shaft

  Flexible-shaft sanding accessories

  Sandpaper, 400- and 220-grit

  Extra-strength glue

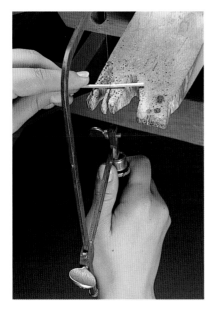

1. Cut a 5 to 6-inch (12.7 to 15.2 cm) length of the wire with the snips or saw as shown. (I usually saw thick-gauge wire; thick metal puts stress on my snips.) You don't have to be too particular about the length. The swirl can be any size you want.

2. Hold one end of the wire in the flat-nose pliers, and bend the other end up to make a small L shape. While holding this L shape in the pliers, completely wrap the wire one time around the mandrel

at your ring size mark as shown. (Since the metal becomes work-hardened and springy, you can make the ring one size smaller.)

3. Using the barrette needle file, file away the tip of the L shape to make the wire thinner at this point (see photo). Keep filing until the smaller pointed peg fits into the pearl or bead hole. Leave some wire thick near the crook of the L shape. You'll need to grasp this when making the swirl.

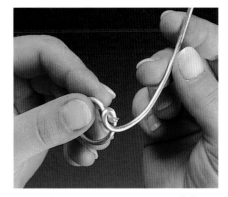

4. Hold onto the L shape with the flat-nose pliers if needed, making sure not to break off the filed peg. Use your fingers to bend the wire around the peg as shown. Spiral the wire to the size you desire. Cut off excess wire length, and sand the cut end.

5. If the pliers left marks on the wire, sand them off with 400-grit paper. Finish the ring as desired. Put a small dot of extra-strength glue on the filed wire end, and gently place the half-drilled pearl or bead on the peg as shown.

Pyramid Necklace

This design allows you to create a chain by interlocking metal elements. Shapes are sawed from copper with a hook on one end and a hole in the other. Decorative chasing marks add a touch of whimsy.

WHAT YOU NEED

- Sheet metal, 18 to 26 gauge
- Steel ruler
- Scribe
- Chasing hammer and punch
- Steel block
- Saw frame and blades
- Needle files
- Flexible shaft
- Flexible-shaft sanding accessories
- Sandpaper, 400- and 220-grit
- Assorted drill bits
- Chasing tools
- Round-nose pliers

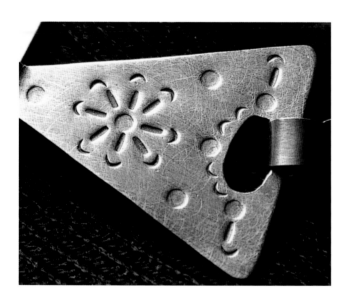

1. Mark the sheet metal into a grid of 35 x 25-mm rectangles. Mark 15 rectangles for a 16-inch (40.6 cm) necklace. Add one or two more rectangles to the grid to make a longer necklace. Use the metal ruler and scribe to draw a horizontal centerline down the length of each

rectangle. Scribe two more lines, one 2 mm above and one 2 mm below the centerline. (This 4-mm space will be used for the link connectors.) Measure 25 mm down the long edge of each rectangle, and mark a vertical line at this point. This creates a 25-mm square within each segment. This is the area in which you'll design the links. This leaves a 4 x 10-mm metal section within which to make the link connectors (see illustration, below left).

2. Design the shape of the links; then, as shown, scribe the shapes inside the 25-mm squares marked in step 1. (It's best for the links to be any shape other than square.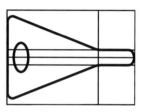
A square prohibits movement of the links. Circles, ovals, or triangles work great in this necklace.) When designing, remember that you must have a hole for threading the connectors. This hole can be any shape that works with your design and allows for movement of the connectors.

3. Saw out each link. File and sand all edges so the lines are clean and even. Pierce and saw out the connector holes (see photo). File and sand the holes.

4. Use the steel block and chasing tools to imprint a design on the links as shown. (I used a variety of handmade stamps and chased my design freehand. You can be as particular or as random as you like.) Apply a patina to the links if desired, sand each to a 400-grit finish, and then give them a final finish.

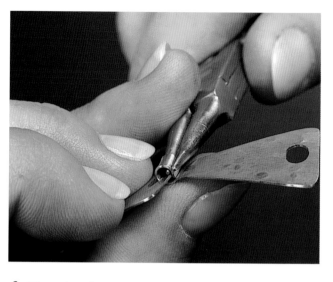

6. Thread each connector into the hole on another link, leaving one link off the chain. Completely and securely close the connectors with the round-nose pliers (see photo). If needed, slightly overlap a circle to ensure a tight connection.

5. Bend up each connector at a 90° angle to the link. Use the round-nose pliers to curl each connector into a circle as shown, but don't close the circle completely now; you'll need an opening to thread each connector into the next link.

7. Make the connector on the unconnected link into a hook for the clasp. Round the hook's end so it looks just like the other links from the top (see photo). Leave the tail straight and thread it into the hole in the last link on the other end of the necklace.

Geometric Bracelet

Chunky, funky, and playful, this bracelet is constructed of several curved metal links. Simple cut-out shapes based on circles and squares make the overall design light and airy. I used multiple jump rings and hooks to give the bracelet plenty of movement and aesthetic appeal.

WHAT YOU NEED

Scribe

Steel ruler

Sheet metal, 24 gauge

Plastic circle and square templates

Saw frame and blades

Needle files

Bastard file

Flexible shaft

Flexible-shaft sanding accessories

Sandpaper, 400- and 220-grit

Chasing hammer and punch

Steel block

Round bracelet mandrel or round mandrel of similar size

Wooden or rawhide mallet

Assorted drill bits

Wire, 16 and 18 gauge

Assorted round mandrels

Round-nose, chain-nose, and flat-nose pliers

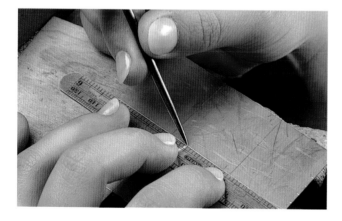

1. Use the scribe and steel ruler to mark the sheet metal into six rectangular sections, or links, each

30 x 35 mm (see photo). This makes a bracelet slightly more than 6¾ inches (17.1 cm) long, including the clasp. If your wrist is larger, make longer links.

2. Use the circle and square templates and the scribe to draw a geometric design on each link. To keep the link designs organized, shade the negative spaces with a marker as shown so you'll know which spaces to saw out. Leave room on each link for the jump-ring holes; the holes must be at least 1.5 mm in from the edge of the metal for strength. (My design uses six jump rings per connection.) Include room for the clasp in the bracelet design. [I used three hooks operating together as one clasp. On one rectangle, I drilled six holes to hold the hook connectors (each clasp has two connectors). On another rectangle, I drilled three larger holes to accommodate the hooks.]

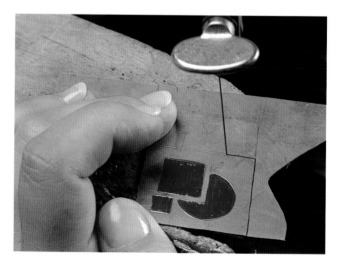

3. Saw out the links (see photo), and then file or sand the edges straight. Dimple the drill marks for the link designs, the jump-ring holes, and the clasp connections.

4. Before drilling and sawing out each link, you'll shape the bracelet. Forming in a solid sheet before piercing and sawing metal ensures each piece has an even curve. (If the metal is formed after the piercing and sawing, the design shapes can become distorted and uneven. This is especially impor-tant when making extremely curved or domed metal pieces.) Hold one link on the bracelet mandrel, and hammer the metal into the curved shape with the rawhide or wooden mallet as shown. Repeat this process on all remaining links.

5. Drill all holes, and saw out the negative shapes (see photo). File the designs with the needle files if needed, or sand. Sand all links to a 400-grit finish. Finish the metal as desired. (I used a coarse-grit steel wool for a shiny finish.)

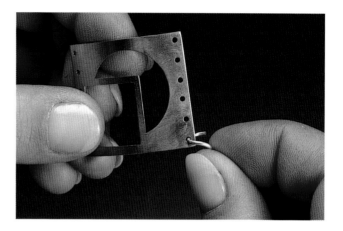

6. Wrap the 16- or 18-gauge wire around an appropri-ately sized mandrel to make at least 24 jump rings for this bracelet. The jump rings must be large enough to span the distance between the link holes. Experiment to find the right jump-ring size (see photo). Also, make sure the drilled holes are large enough to accommodate the jump rings. The jump rings should wiggle in their holes. If the rings don't move, enlarge the holes. (If you drill carefully, you can enlarge drilled holes without having to sand again.) Saw the jump rings apart and set them aside.

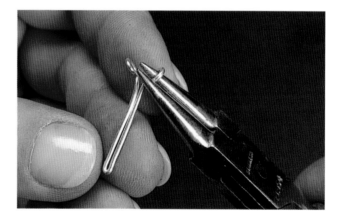

7. To make a clasp hook like the one in my design, cut a length of the 18-gauge wire approximately 3 inches (7.6 cm) long. Bend the wire in half; then use the round-nose pliers to curl each end into a circle (see photo). Pull the circles apart into a V shape so they fit into the drilled holes. Curve the center of the bent wire over to make a hook. Make three clasp hooks this way. Thread the jump rings and the clasp hooks through the drill holes.

Nut-and-Bolt Brooch

This contemporary pin is based on an ancient technique. Throughout the ages, in all parts of the world, the thorn clasp was used like a button to hold material together. The kinetic decorative flowers on this pin are attached to the disc with nuts and bolts: the flowers can move because the width of the metal disc is thinner than the threads on the nuts.

WHAT YOU NEED

Nickel silver sheet metal, 24 gauge

Scribe

Plastic circle template

Steel ruler

Saw frame and blades

Chasing hammer and punch

Steel block

Flexible shaft

Assorted drill bits

Needle files

Bastard file

Flexible-shaft sanding accessories

Sandpaper, 400- and 220-grit

Separators

Photocopied circle divider template, page 21

Wooden dap

Wooden dapping block

Brass sheet metal, 24 gauge

Chasing tools (optional)

Brass wire, 16 gauge

Round-nose pliers

Miniature nuts and bolts (sold at many jewelry
    supply stores)

Flat-nose pliers

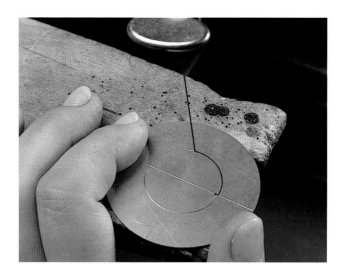

1. Scribe a circle onto the nickel silver, 50 mm in diameter. Mark the circle's x- and y-axes. Using the axis marks as a guide, place the circle template over the marked circle, and scribe a second circle in the center of the first circle, 25 mm in diameter. Pierce and saw out the disc and the inner circle (see photo). File and sand the circle until its exterior and interior edges are smooth.

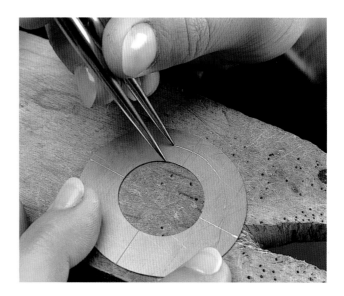

2. Open the separators to 6 mm, exactly half of the width of the metal "washer" made in step 1. Using the outside edge of the washer as a guide, scribe a line around the washer's width as shown to mark its centerline.

5. Using the wooden dap and the chasing hammer, gently hammer the washer into the wooden dapping block's concavity. Depress the washer all the way around its circumference, making the metal disc evenly concave.

3. Use the circle divider template to divide the washer into eight sections. Mark each section, and then dimple the metal at each mark on the centerline for drilling. Drill the metal with a bit that corresponds to the diameter of the miniature nuts (see photo).

6. Design eight decorative elements to attach to the washer. (My pieces look like little flowers, but your shapes can be anything you can imagine as long as they fit within a 13 x 13-mm metal square.) Scribe the designs onto the 24-gauge brass sheet, and saw out. At the center of each decorative element, dimple and then drill a hole the same diameter as the miniature nuts, or slightly larger. Decorate the elements with chasing if you wish. (As shown, I used a blunt-end round chasing tool to dot my flowers.) Sand each decorative element to a 400-grit finish, and then finish as you like. (I used a fine-grit steel wool.)

4. At a point exactly between two of the eight drilled holes, measure 3 mm in from the washer's interior edge as shown, and dimple a drill mark. Drill this hole with a 2-mm bit. (This is where you'll attach the thorn.) Sand the washer to a 400-grit finish, and then finish the metal as you like. (I used a fine-grit steel wool.)

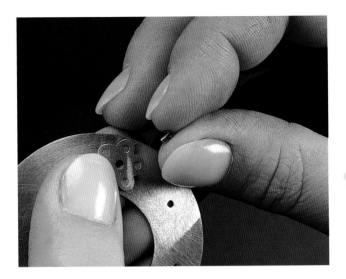

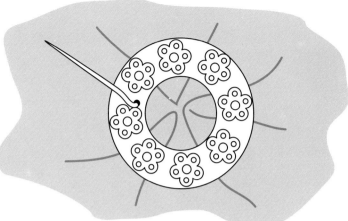

Figure 1

7. Cut a length of the 16-gauge brass wire approximately 50 mm long for the thorn. Use the bastard file to file one end of the thorn to a point that is sharp and tapered enough to pass through loosely woven cloth. Use the round-nose pliers to make a loop at the opposite end of the thorn. Sand the thorn to a 400-grit finish. Attach the decorative elements to the washer with the miniature nuts and bolts (see photo).

8. Thread the looped end of the thorn through the hole drilled in step 4. Tightly close the loop as you would a jump ring. To attach the pin to cloth, pull a piece of cloth through the center hole (figure 1). Put the point of the thorn into the cloth (figure 2), and then pull the cloth back down through the center hole until the pin lies flat (figure 3).

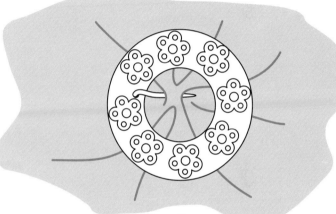

Figure 2

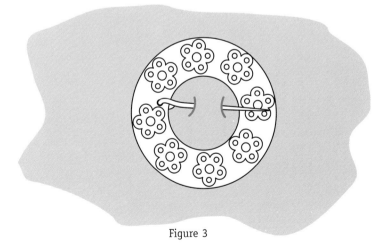

Figure 3

Blooming Rivet Band

Most metal seams are designed to be discreet or disappear entirely, but giving them prominence can produce interesting results. Along with its distinctive overlapped ends, this ring features deeply chased lines, matting, and two prominent split rivets. The ends of the tube are notched with a saw prior to riveting. This extra step gives the rivet its flower shape.

WHAT YOU NEED

Steel ruler

Scribe

Sterling silver sheet metal, 24 gauge

Saw frame and blades

Bastard file

Tape

Steel block

Chasing tools

Chasing hammer and punch

Flexible shaft

Assorted drill bits

Flexible-shaft sanding accessories

Sandpaper, 400- and 220-grit

Sterling tubing, 1.8 mm OD

Wooden or rawhide mallet

Ring mandrel

Chain-nose pliers (optional)

Black patina (optional)

2. Tape the band on top of the steel block and chase the design as shown, remembering that the last 5 mm on each end will be riveted. (I chased straight lines on my band, and then used a matting tool to fill the lines with texture.)

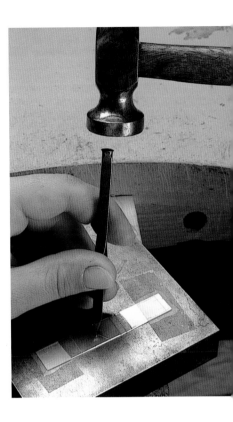

1. Use figure 2 on page 21 to determine the measurement for your ring size. Add 5 mm to this measurement to get the total length for this band. (The extra length provides space for the metal to overlap and be riveted as shown.) The width of the band should be at least 8 mm wide to accommodate the two split rivets. (My band is 12 mm wide.) Use the scribe and steel ruler to mark the band on the sterling sheet metal. Saw out the band, and then use the bastard file to file the edges straight.

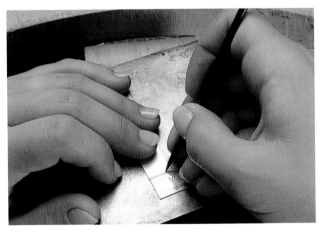

3. Determine the placement of the four rivet holes, two on each end of the band. Measure in equally from both the ends and the edges of the band as shown. (My rivets are 3 mm in from the edges and 2.5 mm in from the ends of my band.) Dimple, and then drill the rivet holes the same diameter as the tubing. Sand the band to a 400-grit finish, keeping the chasing intact.

4. Firmly hold the tubing in your fingers. Saw into the end of the tubing at a 90° angle to cut a slot approximately 2 mm long. Turn the tubing 45°, and cut another 2-mm slot (see photo). Cut the tubing 5 to 6 mm long. Repeat this process to make a second tube to rivet. Sand the ends of both tubes with 400-grit sandpaper.

5. Use the wooden hammer or rawhide mallet and the ring mandrel to form the band into shape. Bend the ring until the four rivet holes align (see photo).

6. Use your fingers or the chain-nose pliers to gently bend out all four sections of the slotted tubing into a flower-like shape (see photo). Insert both tubes into the drilled rivet holes with the flower shapes on the inside of the band.

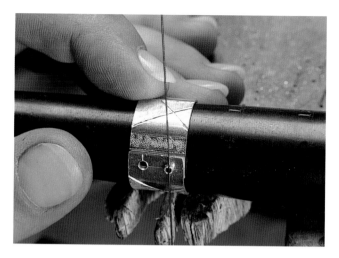

7. Following the process in step 4, saw two slits in each flat tube end as shown. Flare the slit ends into the flower shape, as in step 6. (The rivet holes secure the tubing and provide resistance for sawing.) Place the band back on the ring mandrel, and arrange the split rivet flowers in a pleasing position. Gently hammer the split rivets to secure. Sand the rivets with 400-grit paper to remove all burrs.

8. If you wish to blacken the chasing, make a patina finish on the metal as shown. Sand off the patina on the top metal layer, and finish. (I used a fine steel wool to achieve a satin finish.)

Etched Copper Earrings

It's easy to create this lovely pair of earrings. First, you'll
use the most simple piercing and sawing techniques to
shape the metal. Then, all you have to do is dream up
an interesting relief design, and let the acid do
the rest of the work!

WHAT YOU NEED

Copper sheet metal, 20 gauge or thicker

Scribe

Saw frame and blades

Needle files

Flexible shaft

Flexible-shaft sanding accessories

Sandpaper, 400- and 220-grit

Electric tape or adhesive shelving paper

Craft knife

Baking soda

Ferric chloride*

Small plastic or glass dish with locking lid

Old kitchen scrub or toothbrush

Household abrasive cleanser

Chasing hammer and punch

Steel block

Drill bit, 1 mm

Sterling silver wire, 20 gauge

Round-nose pliers

Snips

*You can buy ferric chloride at computer or electronic stores. It's used to etch computer motherboards.

1. Design a shape for the earrings and simple positive and negative forms to be etched (see photo). Scribe the earring shapes onto the metal, and saw out. File the metal edges, and then sand to a 400-grit finish.

2. Cover the whole surface of both earrings, front and back, with a masking of electrical tape or adhesive shelving paper. Use the craft knife to trim excess masking from around the edges of the metal. Cut out the shapes to be etched from the masking. Use the pointed end of the craft knife to pull up and remove the cut masking as shown.

3. With the baking soda nearby to neutralize any spills, pour some ferric chloride into the small plastic or glass dish. Adhere a long strip of tape across the back of the earrings. The tape must span the diameter of the dish. Hang the earrings upside down in the dish so the copper rests on the surface of the ferric chloride liquid as shown. (Don't immerse the earrings in the liquid; this would cause all exposed copper to be eaten away.) Place the lid on the dish and put it in a safe spot, preferably on a counter or near the floor. It's safest to store or leave acids near the ground so they're less likely to spill. If any acid gets on your skin, wash immediately with cold water and baking soda.

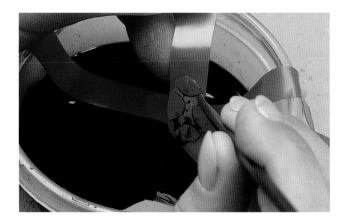

4. Leave the copper to etch for approximately four hours; then check to see if the acid has eaten away enough copper (see photo). A successful etch should be deep enough to show two distinct design layers. If the etch is not deep enough, leave the earrings in the acid dish for another hour, and then recheck the metal. The depth of the etch is up to you. (It can be interesting to leave a piece in the acid until it begins to eat holes through the thickness of the metal. Experiment!)

5. Remove the earrings from the acid, and immediately sprinkle baking soda on the metal. Rub the earrings under water with an old kitchen scrub or toothbrush to remove the acid (see photo). Using the

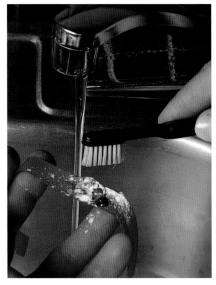

household abrasive cleanser, rub the earrings again. (This step also gives them a bit of shine.) Dry the earrings and place them aside.

Note: If you wish to recycle the acid, either pour it back into the original container, or keep it in a separate container marked "used." Acids lose some of their

power with each etch, so you may want to separate new and old acids. If you wish to dispose of the used acid, first neutralize it by pouring a hefty amount of baking soda into the dish. Do this with plenty of ventilation and over a sink—the solution will bubble up and overflow. After it finishes bubbling, the acid is neutralized, and you can wash your dish or throw it away.

6. Decide where to drill holes for the earwires. Mark the holes, dimple, and drill. Sand the earrings to a 400-grit finish, and then finish as you like. (As shown, I used a green kitchen scrub. A patina also looks wonderful on top of etched metal. If you wish to add color to your metal, do so now.)

7. Follow steps 5 and 6 of the Beaded Dangles on page 33 to make the earwires. Attach the earwires to the earrings (see photo), and then sand the ends of the earwires.

Floating Pearl Ring

The glow of its cool undertones makes sterling silver an impeccable escort for prized gems. Pearls are fashion classics, yet this cold-connected contemporary setting really gives tradition a new twist.

WHAT YOU NEED

Flat or square sterling silver wire, 2.5–5 mm

Scribe

Saw frame and blades

Ring mandrel

Wooden or rawhide mallet

Flat-nose pliers

Steel block

Needle files

Flexible shaft

Flexible-shaft sanding accessories

Sandpaper, 400- and 220-grit

5–7 mm freshwater pearl or bead with large hole

Sterling silver tubing, must fit into bead hole

Chasing hammer and punch

Assorted drill bits

Flaring tool

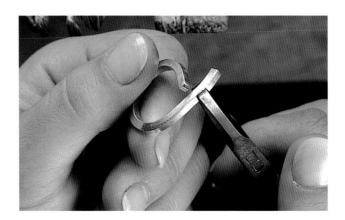

2. With the flat-nose pliers, bend up one end of the wire, making a tail approximately 7 to 8 mm long. Repeat this process on the other wire end as shown. Make this angle as sharp or soft as you like, as long as the bead fits into the space you've created. If the square wire has become warped or distorted, hammer it with the wooden hammer on top of the steel block to make it square again. Check the fit of the ring. Adjust and re-hammer as needed, making sure the bead still fits into the opening. File off all plier marks, and sand the ring to a 220-grit finish.

1. Look at figure 2 on page 21 and find the measurement for your ring size. Cut a length of sterling silver wire approximately 15 mm longer than this measurement. This extra length becomes the part of the ring that holds the bead. Bend the wire around the ring mandrel at the place your ring size is marked. Hammer the ring into shape with the wooden or rawhide mallet (see photo). Make sure the ring fits. If not, pull the wire apart to make it bigger, or push the wire together to make it smaller. Re-hammer the wire into shape on the ring mandrel.

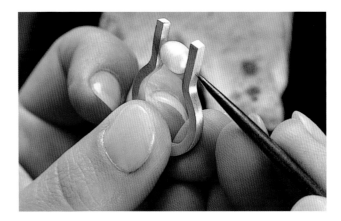

3. Place the bead in the opening, and determine its best position. (You may want the bead to rest against your finger, or you may want to place it higher in the opening.) Mark the spot for the holes that will hold the tubing (see photo). Remove the bead; then dimple and drill holes the same diameter or slightly larger than the tubing.

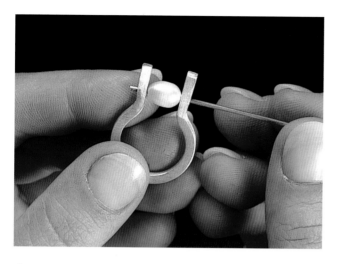

4. Thread the tubing through one drill hole, through the bead, and then through the next drill hole as shown. Mark and then cut the tubing to the appropriate length for riveting. Decide how much wire you want to project above the bead. (If you have enough wire length, you even could stack two beads on top of each other.) Remove the bead and tubing.

6. Rethread the tubing and bead through the rivet holes. Hold the ring flat against the steel block with the curved lower section of the ring hanging over the edge as shown so you don't nick the metal. Rivet both sides of the tubing.

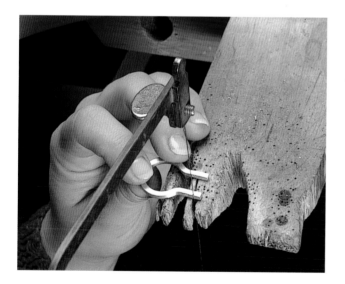

5. Saw the wire end (see photo) and the tubing to the appropriate lengths. Sand the ends of the tubing, and then sand the entire ring to a 400–grit finish. Finish the surface of the ring as desired. (I gave mine a matte finish by hand sanding with 220-grit paper.)

Alternate ring design with bead

Bangle Bracelet

Rectangular wire forms the base of this attractive bracelet that is as comfortable to wear as it is stylish. Tube rivets not only secure the ends together, but also enhance the decorative motif. Spacer tubes set between the wire ends generate the bracelet's architectural feel.

WHAT YOU NEED

Saw frame and blades

Rectangular sterling silver wire, 2 x 5 mm

Needle files

Flexible shaft

Flexible-shaft sanding accessories

Sandpaper, 400- and 220-grit

Separators

Steel ruler

Chasing hammer and punch

Steel block

Drill bits, one 1.87 mm to accommodate tubing

Sterling silver tubing, 1.9 mm ID, 2.6 mm OD*

Sterling silver tubing, 1.85 mm OD*

Wooden or rawhide mallet

Bracelet mandrel

Flaring tool

*The tubing must *telescope*—the smaller tube should fit snugly inside the larger tube.

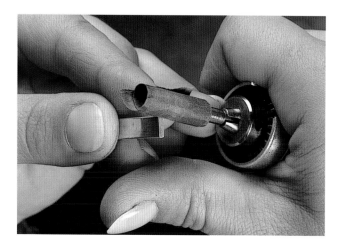

1. Use the saw to cut a piece of the sterling rectangular wire approximately 8¾ inches (22.2 cm) long. [This measurement is for a medium-size bangle. To make a smaller size, subtract 1 inch (2.5 cm) from this measurement, or add 1 inch (2.5 cm) to make a larger size.] File and sand the cut wire ends. Slightly round all the corners with the sanding mandrel as shown.

2. Open the separators to 6 mm. In the center of the flat wire, make a mark 6 mm in from one end of the wire. Make a second, and then a third mark, each 6 mm away from the last (see photo). Make six marks on the other end of the wire. Make the first mark 6 mm in from the one end of the wire. Make five more marks, each 6 mm away from the last. At the marked points, dimple and drill holes the same diameter as the smaller tubing (1.85 mm). Sand the wire to a 400-grit finish.

3. Use the saw to cut three pieces of the larger tubing, each approximately 10 mm long (see photo). Sand the cut ends until they are smooth with no burrs. These 10-mm pieces are the tube separators. Saw three pieces of the smaller tubing, each approximately 13 mm long. Saw three more pieces of the smaller tubing, each approximately 5 mm long. Sand the cut ends. (The 13-mm pieces will be the functional tube rivets, and the 5-mm pieces will be the decorative tube rivets.)

4. Using the rawhide or wooden hammer and the bracelet mandrel, bend the bangle into a circle. Start the bending with your fingers, and then hammer the piece into a firmer round shape (see photo). Don't worry about overlapping the bangle ends yet; just make sure the bangle has a nice round shape.

5. Flare one end of each of the three 13-mm tubes with the flaring tool. Flare the ends as much as you can by gently tapping the flaring tool with your hammer while holding the tubing on top of the steel block as shown.

6. With the flared end facing the inside of the wire, insert one of the 13-mm tubes into the first of the six holes, nearest the end of the wire. Slide one of the 10-mm tube separators over the smaller tube. Pull over the opposite end of the bangle, and thread the unflared end of the functional tube into the third hole (the hole *farthest* from the end of the wire). Put the bangle on the bracelet mandrel, and rivet as shown in the photo, above left. (The bracelet mandrel acts like a steel block and helps the inside rivets become flush.) Tap the inside rivets as needed (see photo, above right). Repeat this process to make the last two rivets, remembering to include the tube separators.

7. Flare one end of each of the three 5-mm tubes cut in step 3. Insert one flared tube into a rivet hole with the flared end on the inside of the bangle (see photo). Place the bangle on the bracelet mandrel, and rivet. Repeat this process for the remaining two decorative rivets. Give the bangle a final finish. (I used the green scrubby for a matte finish.)

Polka-Dot Tube Earrings

Welcome to the world of decorative drilling, an easy
technique with spectacular results. Beads made from
tubing are simple to fashion and look very avant-garde.
Strung with pearls on a capped French wire, these
trés chic earrings soon may become your favorite pair.

WHAT YOU NEED

Sterling silver wire, 20 gauge

Steel ruler

Snips

Round-nose pliers

Saw frame and blades

Sterling silver tubing, less than 3 mm OD

Separators or digital calipers

Scribe

Chasing hammer and punch

Steel block

Flexible shaft

Assorted drill bits

Flexible-shaft sanding accessories

Sandpaper, 400- and 220-grit

Pearls or accent beads of your choice*

Round mandrel, 6 mm

*If the pearls won't fit on the wire, their holes can be enlarged. Coat a bit .9 mm or larger with oil or wax, and drill straight through the existing hole. This method only works with organic materials.

1. Cut two lengths of the silver wire, each 60 mm long, for the earwires and for stringing the tubing and beads. Bend a stop for the earwires as shown. (I made a jump ring, but you can make a swirl, a square, or any shape that accents your design and prevents the tubing and beads from sliding off.)

2. Saw the tubing into four 15-mm sections and four 9-mm sections. This makes a total of four layers of tube "beads" per earring. Using the separators or digital calipers,

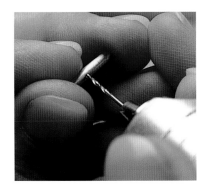

mark the center of each cut tube, and dimple this point. To make the bead hole, hold one cut tube in your fingers, and drill straight through the dimpled point at a 90° angle as shown, below left. (You'll string each tube bead onto the earwires through this hole.) Drill the bead hole through all remaining tubes.

3. Use the scribe to dimple where you wish to make decorative drill holes. Drill these dimples with a small-size bit (see photo). Decide where you'd like bigger holes, and use a larger bit to increase the diameter of the existing holes. Sand each tube bead to a 400-grit fin-

ish, including all cut ends. String the tube beads onto the earwires however you wish. (I alternated the tube beads with pearls.)

4. At the top of the beads, bend the earwire flat toward you (see photo), and then back away from you around a round mandrel, approximately 6 mm in diameter. Snip the ends of the earwire so they're long enough not to fall out of the ear, but short enough not to rub the neck. (My earwires are about 23 mm long.) Sand the ends of the earwire, and finish. (I used a green kitchen scrub for a matte finish.)

Screen Earrings

Jewelry making lends itself to the creative mixing of all types of materials. Sparkly cubic zirconias lose none of their appeal when veiled behind black plastic window screen. You also can trap found objects under the screens such as pebbles or shark's teeth. Two metal frames secured with tube rivets sandwich the decorative elements together and accommodate the earwire.

WHAT YOU NEED

Sterling silver sheet metal, 24 gauge

Steel ruler

Scribe

Saw frame and blades

Bastard file

Plastic circle template

Chasing hammer and punch

Steel block

Flexible shaft

Flexible-shaft sanding accessories

Sandpaper, 400- and 220-grit

Assorted drill bits

Sterling silver tubing, 1.6 mm OD

Plastic window screen

Round faceted stone, 6.5 mm in diameter

Flaring tool

Sterling silver wire, 20 gauge

Round-nose pliers

Chain-nose pliers

2. Using the circle template and the center points as your guides, scribe a 5-mm circle onto two of the squares and a 14-mm circle onto the remaining squares. Pierce and saw out these circles as shown. (The *culet*, or pointed part of the stone, will rest in the 5-mm circle.) File and sand the circles so they're perfectly round.

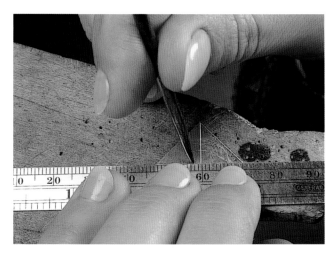

1. Measure and mark four squares on the 24-gauge sterling silver sheet metal, each 17 x 17 mm. Saw out the squares, and file their edges straight. Find the center of each square by making two lines that cross the square from one corner to the opposite corner in an X shape (see photo). The point where the lines intersect is the center of the square.

3. On the two metal squares with the larger sawed-out circles (the front earring squares), mark the holes for the tube rivets. Using the original center point guidelines, measure in 2.5 mm from each corner of both squares. Dimple this point with the scribe. First drill this mark with a small drill bit, and then enlarge the hole to the size of the tubing as shown, approximately 1.6 mm. Repeat this process for all eight holes on the two front earring squares. Sand all four squares, back and front, to a 400-grit finish; then apply any finish you desire. (I finished mine with 220-grit sandpaper.)

4. Saw eight lengths of tubing for the rivets as shown, each about 3 mm long. Sand the cut ends. Safely place these rivets aside.

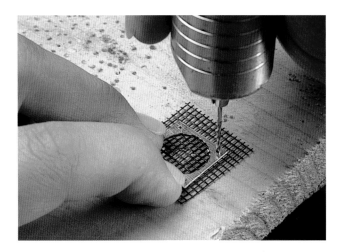

5. Assemble the metal squares in two sets, each with one front and one back piece. Sandwich a piece of the plastic screening between each set of squares. (The screening can be larger than the squares; any extra can be cut off later.) Tightly hold the squares together, dimple, and then drill two holes in diagonal corners as shown. Make the holes the same size as the tubing. Drill right through the screen and the metal.

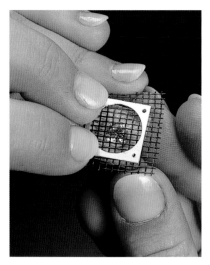

6. Thread a long piece of tubing into one earring corner, passing through both metal squares and the screen. This tube holds everything in place while the stone is gently and slowly manipulated into place. Keep the metal flat as you trap the stone under the screen and front square (see photo). Once the stone is snug in its hole, realign the drill holes and pull the screen at its edges. The screen should be tight under the metal. Rivet the two drilled corners on each earring. Dimple, drill the remaining corner holes, insert the tubes, and rivet to secure.

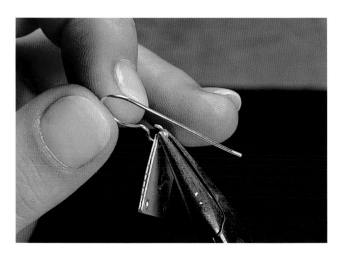

7. Cut off any excess screen from the earring edges with scissors or a craft knife. File the edges again to make them even and flush. Gently round the corners of the earrings with the file. Sand all edges to a 400-grit finish. To make the earwires, follow steps 5 and 6 of the Beaded Dangles on page 33. Attach the earwires to the earrings through one of the tube rivets as shown.

Sunburst Posts

Designing a pair of earrings without soldering on the posts
was an enticing challenge. My solution was to layer the post's
pad between two sheet metal discs, and then rivet all three
elements in place. The contour of the front disc features
a sunburst motif which is enhanced by fine saw
lines on the rear disc.

WHAT YOU NEED

Plastic circle template

Scribe

Steel ruler

Sterling silver sheet metal, 24 gauge

Photocopied circle divider template, page 21

Saw frame and blades

Needle files

Chasing hammer and punch

Steel block

Flexible shaft

Assorted drill bits

Flexible-shaft sanding accessories

Sandpaper, 400- and 220-grit

Sterling silver tubing, 1.15 mm OD

Sterling silver earring posts with 5-mm pad

Flaring tool

Ear nuts

2. Dimple the center point on each 1-inch (2.5 cm) disc. Drill a hole for the earpost to fit through as shown. (My earposts are .7 mm in diameter, so I drilled a .73-mm hole.)

3. On each of the four discs, use the steel ruler to draw two parallel lines, each 5 mm away from the x-axis. Draw two more parallel lines on each of the four discs, each 5 mm away from the y-axis.

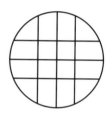

This makes a centered, 10-mm square on the discs (see illustration). The corners of the squares indicate where to drill for the tube rivets. Dimple and drill all four holes only on the ¾-inch (1.9 cm) discs. Drill holes the same size as the tubing, 1.15 mm in diameter. On the 1-inch (2.5 cm) discs, dimple and drill a hole at any one corner of the scribed 10-mm box. These holes help you center the ¾-inch (1.9 cm) discs on top of the 1-inch (2.5 cm) discs.

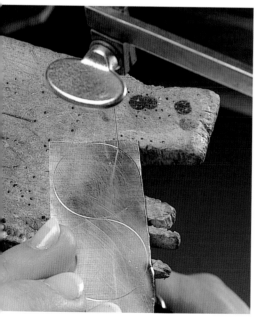

1. Use the circle template and scribe to draw two ¾-inch (1.9 cm) circles and two 1-inch (2.5 cm) circles on the 24-gauge silver sheet metal. Mark the centers of each circle with the scribe by using the photocopied circle divider template as a guide and drawing its x- and y-axes. Saw out the discs (see photo), and file their edges smooth.

4. Using the circle template as a guide, scribe a circle onto each 1-inch (2.5 cm) disc. This circle should be at least 2 mm away from the rivet holes, about 15 mm in diameter.

Staying outside the circle, saw out a decorative edge on the ¾-inch (1.9 cm) discs as shown on the previous page, bottom right. (I cut out triangles, but you could do scalloped edges, wavy edges, or any design that strikes your fancy.) File or sand the sawed edges. Sand both the front and the back of the ¾-inch (1.9 cm) discs to a 400-grit finish.

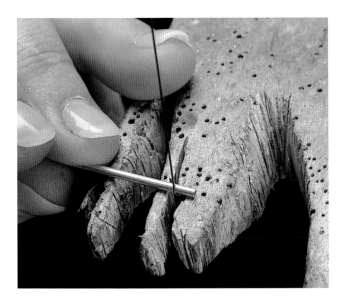

5. Cut eight pieces of tubing (see photo), each 3 mm long, to use as rivets. Sand all cut ends.

6. On the 1-inch (2.5 cm) discs, dimple the corner of the scribed square opposite the hole drilled in step 3 (see photo). Thread a piece of tubing through one hole in the top ¾-inch (1.9 cm) disc and through the drilled hole in the 1-inch (2.5 cm) disc. Using the dimple on the 1-inch (2.5 cm) disc as a guide, line up the corners of the scribed square, and drill a hole through the dimple.

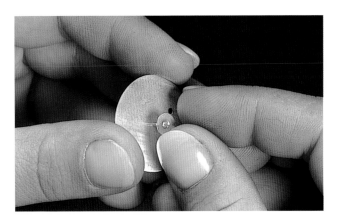

7. Sand the 1-inch (2.5 cm) discs to a 400-grit finish. Thread the earring post with the 5-mm pad into the center hole in the 1-inch (2.5 cm) discs as shown. Place the ¾-inch (1.9 cm) discs on top of the pad. Align the rivet holes, and rivet the opposite sides of the scribed squares. Using the remaining two holes as guides, drill through the 1-inch (2.5 cm) discs, and rivet.

8. Saw decorative edges on the 1-inch (2.5 cm) discs as shown. Leave enough room from the edge of the bottom discs to the edge of the top discs to indicate that there are two layers of metal. (I used saw lines as decoration, but you can saw any design you wish.) File or sand the edges of the 1-inch (2.5 cm) discs. Give the earrings a final finish (I rubbed mine with 220-grit sandpaper), and then put the ear nuts on the earrings.

Layered Cuff Bracelet

The appearance of metal is ever-changing as it reflects light and plays off surrounding colors. To exemplify this characteristic, I designed this multi-tiered, heavily chased cuff with a variety of metals. You can personalize my basic design to suit your own taste or the latest style.

WHAT YOU NEED

Assorted sheet metals, 18 to 26 gauge

Scribe

Metal ruler

Saw frame and blades

Needle files

Bastard file

Flexible shaft

Flexible-shaft sanding accessories

Sandpaper, 400- and 220-grit

Matting or chasing tools

Chasing hammer and punch

Steel block

Assorted drill bits

Oval or round bracelet mandrel

Wooden or rawhide mallet

Sterling silver tubing

Flaring tool

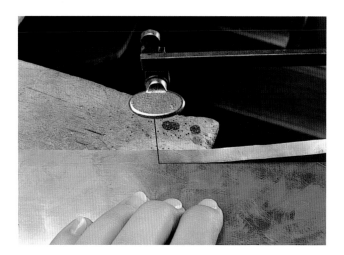

2. Decide what metals you wish to use for the top three cuff layers. (I used two strips of copper and one of silver. These metal strips can be any gauge, preferably under 26 gauge for strength.) Saw each metal piece into a strip as shown, making sure the combined width of the strips is 1 inch (2.5 cm) or less. (My strips are 7 mm, 10 mm, and 3 mm wide.) Make the strips long enough to rest above the cuff. (In descending order, my strips are 190 mm, 180 mm, and 170 mm long.) File or sand each strip so all edges are straight and even.

1. Mark a piece of 18-gauge metal into a 5³/₄ x 1-inch (14.6 x 2.5 cm) rectangle, and saw out. File or sand the edges completely straight; then slightly round and smooth the corners with the bastard file as shown.

3. Use the matting or chasing tools to pattern each strip. [I made hammer marks on one strip with a chasing hammer. On another, I used the end of an old screwdriver to make a random pattern (see photo). On the third strip I hammered the round side of an old file to imprint the file's teeth marks.]

4. At a point approximately 3 mm in from both ends of each strip, mark and dimple drill holes for the tube rivets. Make sure the drill holes on the wide cuff fit the widths of the strips. To do this, first drill holes in the center of each strip end (see photo). Lay the strips side by side on top of the cuff, and mark the drill holes on the cuff. Drill all holes, and sand each strip to a 400-grit finish. Finish each strip surface as you desire. (A patina would enhance the chasing on this bracelet.)

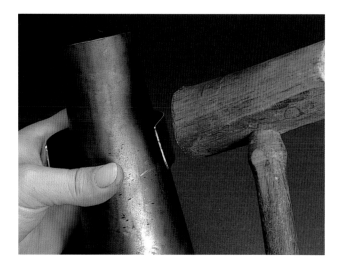

5. Hammer the cuff into shape as shown, using the wooden or rawhide mallet and the oval bracelet mandrel. (If you don't have an oval bracelet mandrel, hammer the cuff around a round bracelet mandrel, and then use your fingers or pliers to give the cuff an oval shape.) Hammering also gives the cuff spring. Sand the cuff to a 400-grit finish, and then finish the cuff surface as desired.

6. Taking into consideration the thickness of the metal layers to be riveted, cut six lengths of sterling silver tubing for the rivets (see photo). Cut each tube rivet between 4 and 5 mm, and sand the ends.

7. Pre-flare one end of the tube rivets. This end rests on the inside of the cuff. Rivet each metal strip onto one end of the cuff (see photo). Instead of using the flat steel block, rivet on top of the steel bracelet mandrel so the metal won't distort in shape. (If you don't have an oval bracelet mandrel, you can rivet on the thin part of a round bracelet mandrel.)

Strips joined to cuff end with tube rivets

8. Take the shortest metal strip, cross it over to the opposite hole on the other end of the cuff, and rivet. Cross the next longest metal strip over to the other end of the bracelet, and rivet. Rivet the longest strip into the remaining hole (see photo). This procedure is up to you; you can cross the strips in whatever fashion you like, or you can leave them straight. However, if you cross the strips, always start with the shortest, and end with the longest strip.

Strips crossed at different heights above cuff

Ladder Choker

Heavy-gauge wires, both straight and twisted, are the
star attraction of this dramatic necklace and pendant
combination. A single wire piece is curved by hand to
fit around the neck; then the wire ends are bent to form
the hook and clasp. The pendant and bales are
assembled with precise wire rivets.

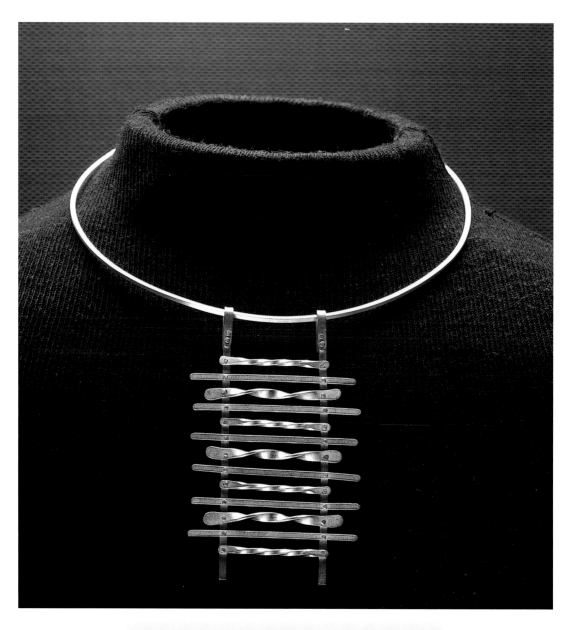

WHAT YOU NEED

Square sterling silver wire, 1.75 mm

Steel ruler

Saw frame and blades

Round-nose pliers

Flexible shaft

Flexible-shaft sanding accessories

Sandpaper, 400- and 220-grit

Wooden or rawhide hammer

Steel block

Square sterling silver wire, 2.5 mm

Rectangular sterling silver wire, 1 x 3.5 mm

Chasing hammer and punch

Drill bit, 1 mm

Sterling silver wire, 18 gauge

Flat-nose pliers

Rectangular sterling silver wire, 1 x 2.5 mm

Separators

2. Use the saw to cut two 85-mm lengths of the 2.5-mm square wire. Straighten and flatten the square wires by hammering them on the steel block with the wooden or rawhide mallet (see photo). Sand the wire ends to remove all burrs.

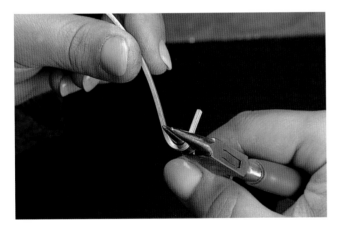

1. To make the neck wire, cut a 15½-inch (39.4 cm) length of the 1.75-mm square wire. Bend the wire into a circle with your fingers until it's perfectly round. With the round-nose pliers, bend the ends of the wire into a U shape as shown so they hook together. (I bent one end to the side and the other end down.) Sand the wire ends with 400-grit sandpaper to remove burrs. Use the wooden or rawhide mallet to hammer the necklace flat on top of the steel block.

3. Cut two 30-mm lengths of the 1 x 3.5-mm rectangular wire to use as the bales. Measure in 5 mm, and then 8 mm from both ends of both wires. Mark and dimple these eight points. Use a 1-mm bit to drill through each mark (see photo). Sand the ends of the bale wires. (I rounded my ends, but keep yours square if you like.)

4. On each 85-mm length of square wire cut and prepared in step 2, measure in 4 mm from one end and mark for drilling (see photo). Dimple, and then drill these two holes with the 1-mm bit.

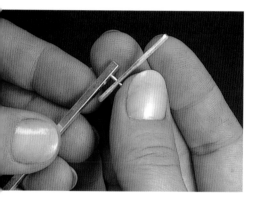

5. Cut four pieces of the 18-gauge round wire, each approximately 5 to 5.5 mm long, to use as rivets for the bale. Sand or file the cut ends flat. Insert one rivet wire into the second hole drilled on the 30-mm-long wire piece as shown. Insert the same rivet wire into the first hole on one 2.5-mm square wire. Bend over the bale wire until its second hole on the opposite end meets up with the rivet wire. Insert the rivet wire through this hole, and rivet. Repeat this process for the second bale. Drill through the 2.5-mm wire to make a hole that aligns exactly with the two unriveted holes on the bale. Thread rivet wires through these holes, and rivet. The bales are now in place.

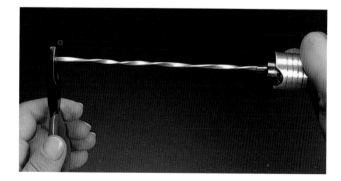

6. Cut a piece of 1.75-mm square wire approximately 12 inches (30.5 cm) long. Insert one wire end into the flexible shaft, and tighten the chuck key until the tool firmly grips the wire. Tightly hold the other end of the wire with the flat-nose pliers. Slowly depress the flexible shaft's foot pedal, and let the wire twist (see photo, below left). Make a loose twist or a tight twist; the choice is yours. Repeat this process with the 1 x 35-mm flat wire. Leave the 1 x 2.5-mm wire flat.

7. Design the structural arrangement of the pendant. (On my pendant the 2.5-mm wires that hold the bales are about 30 mm apart. I used 13 cross wires, each spaced 6 mm apart. Your pendant can be wider or thinner with any number of cross wires.) Use the saw to cut lengths of the twisted wire for the cross wires (see photo). They all can be the same length, or you can vary the lengths as I did. (My cross wires extend past the edges of the 2.5-mm square base wires, but you may want yours flush.) Whatever your cross-wire design, remember to include space for the rivets.

8. Use the chasing hammer and the steel block to gently hammer the ends of all twisted cross wires flat before riveting as shown in the photo to the right. Carefully

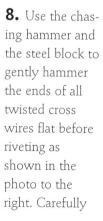

mark, dimple, and drill rivet holes on only one end of each cross wire (see photo, left). Drill the holes with a 1-mm bit to fit the 18-gauge riveting wire.

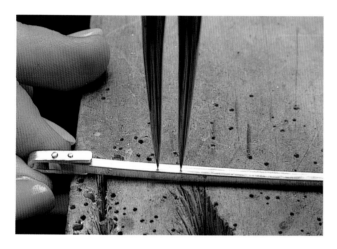

9. Use the separators to draw a centerline down the length of both base wires. Using the separators to make precise equal measurements, mark (see photo), dimple, and drill the rivet holes down both of the 2.5-mm square base wires.

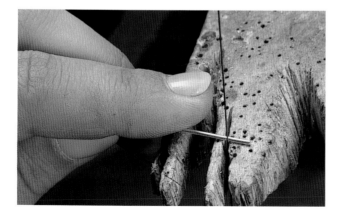

10. Cut as many rivet wires as needed to secure the cross wires on both sides of the pendant (see photo).

Make each rivet wire approximately 5 to 5.5 mm long. It's a good idea to cut a few extra rivet wires in case of mistakes or if some get lost.

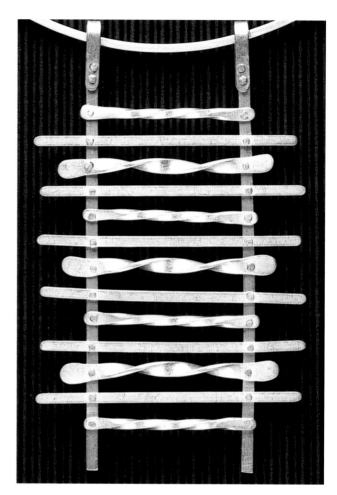

11. Rivet the top cross wire onto one base wire. Drill the other side of the cross wire and rivet it to the second base wire. Your pendant is now held together by the "top rung of the ladder." Rivet the next cross wire to the base wire on one side, drill the hole on the opposite side (using the first cross-wire hole as a guide), and rivet. Continue this process until all cross wires are riveted in place. This is a tedious process, because you must fully rivet one cross wire at a time to ensure all holes properly align. DO NOT drill all the second cross-wire rivet holes at once; you definitely will run into trouble with misaligned holes. Give the pendant and neck wire a final finish; then thread the pendant on the neck wire.

Cone-Top Rivet Ring

Your design for the top of this ring can be as classic or as flamboyant as you desire. The basic band is composed of three metal layers held together by wire rivets. Contrasting the colors of the sheet metal and wire makes the ring a real attention-getter.

WHAT YOU NEED

Plastic circle template

Scribe

Sheet metal, 24 gauge or thicker

Steel ruler

Chasing hammer and punch

Steel block

Flexible shaft

Drill bit, 1 mm

Saw frame and blades

Bastard file

Needle files

Sandpaper, 400- and 220-grit

Separators

Photocopied circle divider template, page 21

Flexible-shaft sanding accessories

Wire, 18 gauge

2. Design and scribe the outside shape of the ring around the inner circle as shown. (I suggest you make the band 4 mm thick or less. Otherwise, the ring will be too wide and uncomfortable on the sides and bottom. (My band is 2 mm wide. My ring design gets funky by poking up from the top of the finger.)

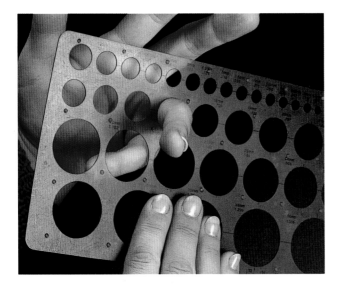

1. Use the plastic circle template to find the measurement for the inside of the ring. Insert your finger in its holes until you find the one that fits (see photo). Scribe this circle onto one sheet of metal, leaving plenty of room around the edges for the ring's outside design.

3. Pierce and saw out the first layer of the ring. Clean up its edges with the files and sandpaper. This is the template for the other ring layers. Trace the outside of the top ring layer onto two other sheets of metal (see photo). You can alternate metal colors or use just one. (This ring can be interesting in many ways—the choice is yours. I used brass and sterling silver with decorative brass rivets. You could use more than three metal layers, but I suggest a three-layer minimum for this project. For an interesting effect, use metals of different thicknesses.) Saw out all metal layers outside the scribe line so you'll have room later to file the layers flush.

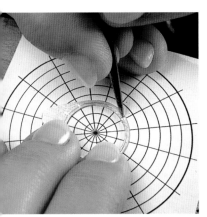

4. On the top ring layer, draw a centerline around the band using the separators and the inside circle as your guide. Make this line exactly half the width of the band or at least 1 mm from its inside edge to leave room for the rivets. Using the photocopied circle divider template, mark the places for the rivets equal distances apart as shown. (My ring has seven rivets. You can use as many as you wish with a minimum of four rivets for strength.) Dimple, and then drill the rivet holes on the top ring layer.

5. Align the drilled top ring layer with the second layer. Tightly hold these together, and drill two rivet holes at opposite points on the band (see photo). Repeat this process for all layers.

6. File and finish the outside edges of each ring layer as shown. If the outside edges are not flush, it's easiest to even them now. The inside edges will be adjusted later, after sawing out the rest of the centers. Sand each

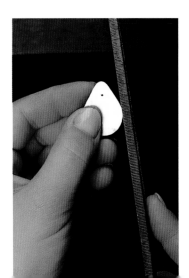

layer to a 400-grit finish, and finish as desired. (I used a dry green kitchen scrub for my final matte finish. A ring with a matte finish quickly turns shiny from wear, so the finish will need daily tending. Much as one has to constantly shine a ring to keep it from tarnishing, the opposite it true here.)

7. Cut the rivet wires approximately 1.5 to 2 mm longer than the total thickness of the ring. Rivet the ring layers together through the two holes drilled in step 5 (see photo). Now you have a secure guide for the rest of the drilling and riveting. Finish riveting the ring together two holes at a time.

8. Drill through, and then carefully saw out the center of the ring, using the top layer as a guide. Hold the saw at a precise 90° angle as you saw out the center part (see photo). This is important for making the inside of the ring even. (If you're concerned about sawing at an exact angle, you can saw inside the line and leave extra metal to file off later.) Once most of the metal is removed from the ring's hole, use the half-round needle

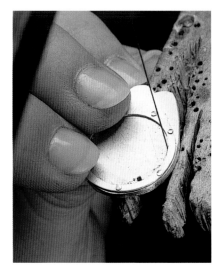

file to file the circle flush. Sand the inside edges with 220-grit, and then 400-grit sandpaper. Touch the rivets with the sanding instrument to smooth away any points or snags.

Pendant with Prong-Set Cabochon

If setting stones sounds difficult to you, this project will change your mind.
These prongs are cut out and bent up from a piece of sheet metal.
Slip your stone into the setting, secure it with the prongs, and you've
got a highly professional-looking pendant.

WHAT YOU NEED

Scribe

Sheet metal, 24 gauge

Saw frame and blades

Needle files

Flexible shaft

Flexible-shaft sanding accessories

Sandpaper, 400- and 220-grit

Round or oval cabochon stone, at least
    15 mm in diameter

Gem template

Photocopied circle divider template, page 21

Steel ruler

Chasing hammer and punch

Steel block

Assorted drill bits

Bastard file

Needle files

Wire, 16 gauge

Flat-nose pliers

Needle-nose pliers

Round mandrel or assorted mandrels

Chain-nose pliers

top metal layer with prongs

back metal layer

cabochon stone

1. Base your pendant on my design (see illustration) or create one of your own. The pendant has three major components: the back metal layer, the top metal layer,

and the cabochon stone. The top layer and the bottom layer trap the cabochon. If you wish, you can use more than two layers for decoration. (My pendant has a bottom layer of nickel silver and a top layer of sterling silver.) Make the bottom layer at least 8 mm larger than the top layer to allow room for the bale holes. Scribe the designs onto the metal, and then saw out the layers. File and sand their edges.

Variation: It would be fantastic to pierce and saw a shape out of the bottom metal layer that would be hidden from view by the stone. This design could make the pendant reversible, or just be a neat secret for the wearer.

2. Scribe the shape of the cabochon in the center of the top metal layer. Since the cabochon is round or oval, use a gem template to draw its shape instead of tracing the actual stone (see photo). Fit the stone into the hole that corresponds to its size, and then move up one size larger on the template. This extra space allows for enough metal to construct and bend up the prongs.

3. Find the x- and y-axis of the top layer, and scribe these lines on the top metal layer. Using the photo-copied circle template as a guide, evenly divide the space between the x- and y-axis into eight sections to make the prongs. (You could make as few as four prongs.) I made oval prongs, but you can make square-, wavy-, or scallop-edged shapes, as long as they're rectangular in form and based on the template lines. Scribe the prongs onto the metal as shown.

4. To determine the length of the prongs, look for the point on the stone where its curved edge rises to become its top surface. Measure this distance and add 2 to 3 mm for total prong length. (Mine are each 6 mm long.) Pierce the top metal layer, and saw out the prongs as shown. File and sand the edges smooth.

5. Mark the rivet points on the top metal layer. (I used eight rivets. They're both functional and decorative. My rivets are about 3.5 mm in from the edges of the top layer. I placed my rivets on the same guidelines used to lay out the prongs.) Dimple, and then drill the rivet holes in the top layer as shown, using a bit that corresponds to 16-gauge round wire, about 1.3 mm in diameter. Sand both metal layers to a 400-grit finish, and apply any final finish you desire.

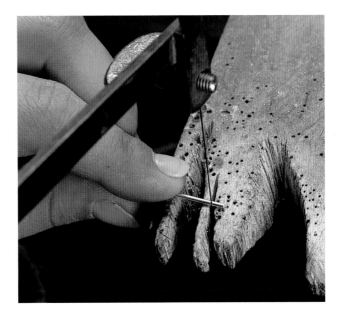

6. Saw the 16-gauge rivet wire into eight pieces, each 3 to 4 mm long (see photo). Sand or file the wire ends flat.

7. Center the top metal layer on the bottom layer. While tightly holding the two layers together, drill rivet holes in two opposite corners. Rivet these two holes as shown. Drill rivet holes in the remaining opposite corners, two at a time, and rivet until all rivets are in place. Sand the rivet heads smooth.

8. Near the top edge of the bottom metal layer, drill two bale holes about 10 to 15 mm apart (see photo). Make each bale hole about 2 mm in diameter so the chain can move freely. Sand as needed, and then return the metal surface to the desired finish.

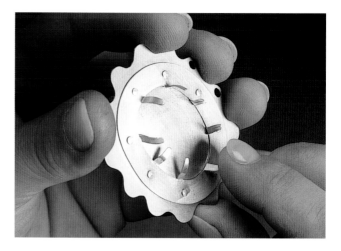

9. Use your fingers or the flat-nose pliers to gently pull the prongs up to a 90° angle (see photo). It's helpful to use the flat-nose pliers to make a nice bend at the base of the prong. Take care not to overbend the metal and break off the prongs; after repeated bending metal eventually becomes so brittle it breaks. With the prongs bent up, the thickness of the metal causes the base of the prong to stick out about 1 mm from the cabochon opening. This is why you drew a shape one size larger than the stone.

10. Place the cabochon inside the prongs. Use your fingers to bend the prongs over the stone. To get the prongs as close to the stone as possible, gently grip each prong with the needle-nose pliers and move the prong back and forth from side to side (see photo). This action is similar to opening and closing jump rings.

11. Use the round wire to create a jump-ring chain. There is no set number of jump rings; you may need to make more as you construct the chain, depending on the mandrel size and wire thickness. (I made my jump rings from 16-gauge wire so the chain looks and feels heavy. My mandrel is about 3.5 mm in diameter. I made about 140 jump rings for a 15½-inch (39.4 cm) necklace. I don't recommend making this chain out of wire thinner than 16 gauge; the connections would be too weak.) Create a clasp by bending 16-gauge wire into a hook shape as shown, with a circle on the end to attach the clasp to the chain. Use a jump ring with a larger diameter for the hook, or use a jump ring on the chain as a hook. If you use a commercial clasp, make sure the 16-gauge wire fits into its hole.

12. To attach the chain to the pendant, make two slightly larger jump rings and thread them through the bale holes. Attach the two large jump rings to

two jump rings in the middle of the chain as shown. Alternately, you can create the chain in two halves and attach the last jump ring on each half directly into the bale holes (see project variation below).

Alternate pendant and chain design

87

Mandala Bracelet

Mandalas have been worn through the ages as amulets for personal protection. Their swelling, symmetrical design conveys a timeless beauty. Create your own special mandala using symbols that are meaningful to you, or use my pattern if you wish.

WHAT YOU NEED

Plastic circle template or separators

Scribe

Sheet metal, 24 gauge

Saw frame and blades

Bastard file

Photocopied mandala pattern, below right

Photocopied circle divider template, page 21

Chasing hammer and punch

Steel block

Flexible shaft

Drill bit, 1 mm

Needle files

Flexible-shaft sanding accessories

Sandpaper, 400- and 220-grit

Metal tubing, 1 mm ID, OD variable
    (mine is 1.85 mm OD)

Sterling silver wire, 18 gauge

Clear tape (optional)

Rectangular sterling silver wire, 1.5 x 6 mm

Bracelet mandrel

Wooden or rawhide mallet

Round-nose or flat-nose pliers

Note: This bracelet is made in two sections: the top decorative half and the bracelet band. By making the top half first, you'll have an easier time later determining the length of the bracelet band.

1. Using a circle template or the separators, scribe two identical discs onto the 24-gauge sheet metal. I suggest beginning with a disc at least 1½ inches (3.8 cm) in diameter. [Mine is 1¾ inches (4.4 cm) in diameter.] Very carefully saw out the discs as shown. Careful sawing eliminates excess filing which can distort the shape of the discs. Use the bastard file to file the disc edges at a 90° angle.

2. Transfer, and then scribe the mandala pattern onto one disc. (The more shapes your mandala has, the less precise your drawing must be. The eye won't recognize small differences in the measurements; it will first

look at the design as a whole.) To mark off equal segments on the disc, use the photocopied circle divider template. Scribe circles of descending diameter on the metal by matching up the template's x- and y-axis. Scribe as many circles as you need to help you plot the mandala design. Make sure to scribe a circle 3 mm in from the disc's edge. Mark eight equally-spaced places for rivets on this circle.

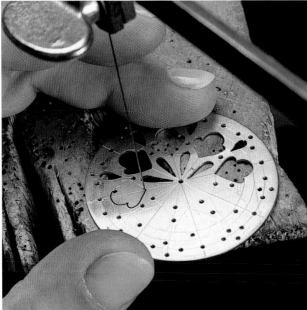

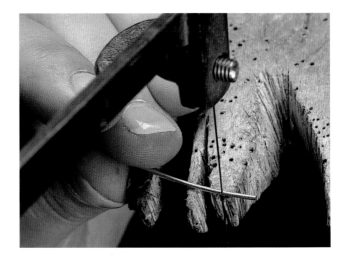

4. Decide how much space you wish to leave between the two discs. (My layers are 5 mm apart.) Saw the tubing into nine pieces of the determined length to use as separators (see photo). File or sand the cut ends flat. Cut the 18-gauge wire into nine sections to use as rivets, each about 3 to 3.5 mm longer than the tubing separators. (My wire pieces are each about 8.5 mm long.) This measurement includes the thickness of the two metal sheets (about 1 mm total). File or sand the cut wire ends flat. Place the wire rivets and tube separators aside.

5. Before riveting the two discs together, you'll need to saw out holes on the bottom disc for the band connection and the clasp. Using the circle divider template as a guide, scribe the x-axis onto the bottom disc.

About 3 mm in from one edge of the disc, draw a rectangle on the scribed line about 1.5 mm larger than the band wire. Repeat this step to draw another rectangle 3 mm in from the opposite edge of the disc. Pierce and saw out these two small symmetrical rectangles

3. Mark, dimple, and drill all holes as shown in top photo. Use a 1-mm drill bit for the rivet holes to match the 18-gauge wire. Pierce and saw out all the shapes (see photo, above). File any irregular shapes with the needle files. Sand the front and the back of the disc with 220-grit and 400-grit paper to remove all scribe marks.

(see photo, page 90, bottom right), and then file them to make sure their lines are straight. Sand the bottom disc using 220-grit and 400-grit paper.

6. Place the top disc on the bottom disc, and align the rectangular holes cut in step 5 between two rivet holes. Tightly hold the discs together or tape them so they won't shift. Using the 1-mm bit, drill two holes on opposite sides of the discs. (The bit passes through the two existing rivet holes, and then the metal of the bottom disc.) Feed one 18-gauge rivet wire through one hole on the bottom disc. Thread the tube separator onto this rivet wire. Feed the remaining wire through the hole in the top disc, and rivet (see photo). Repeat this process on the opposite side of the disc.

7. Using the rivet holes on the top disc as a guide, drill two more opposite holes in the bottom disc. Drill through the existing holes, making sure to keep the drill bit at a 90° angle to the bottom disc. Rivet the rest of the piece as shown, two opposite holes at a time, remembering to include the tube separators and to rivet the center hole. (To ensure equal rivet distances, it's best to make the first two rivets at 12 o'clock and 6 o'clock, and then at 3 o'clock and 9 o'clock, and so on for all eight outside rivets.)

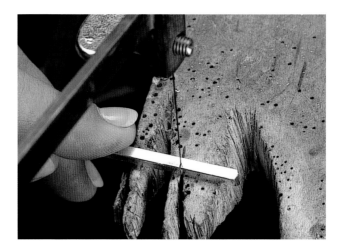

8. Measure your wrist with a piece of wire or string. To determine the length of the band wire, add 1½ inches (3.8 cm) to your wrist measurement, and then subtract the diameter of the mandala. This measurement leaves enough wire length to make the catch and the joint and to give the bracelet room to move around your wrist. Saw the band wire to this length as shown. Sand the wire ends.

9. File both ends of the square wire into a thinner V shape (see photo). Taper the edges of the V beginning about 10 to 13 mm from the end of the wire. Square off the point of the V to approximately 1.5 mm wide. This allows the wire to fit into the rectangles on the bottom disc and allows you to bend the wire with ease.

closing the U, thread it through one of the rectangular holes in the bottom disc. To completely close the U, move the wire back and forth as if you were closing a jump ring.

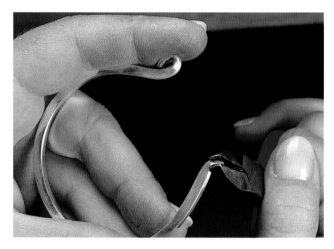

10. Use the bracelet mandrel and the wooden or rawhide mallet to hammer the wire into shape. Hammer hard to harden the metal without distorting the wire shape and give the metal spring. Continue to shape the bracelet as needed with your fingers or pliers as shown. (If you use pliers, wrap their jaws with tape to prevent marking the metal.) Test the spring of the wire by pushing it together. Hammer the wire some more if needed, and then retest. Repeat this process until the metal is well-hardened and springy.

12. Using the round-nose pliers, gently curve the catch end of the band wire as shown. Start with a small curve, and test-fit it in the remaining hole in the bottom disc. Keep bending the wire until it catches in the hole and won't fall out. To make this work properly, you may need to file off some of the wire width or readjust the band shape. Test the metal's spring again to make sure the clasp operates properly. (I usually have to slightly open up the band to give it room for the spring to work.) Sand the band to a 400-grit finish, and then complete the bracelet as you like. (My bracelet is finished with a medium-grit steel wool. A patina would look splendid on this bracelet, too.)

11. Use the pliers to curve one end of the wire for the joint (see photo). This joint isn't a perfect circle. It should look more like a closed U. Before completely

Art Deco Brooch

A properly functioning catch and joint are essential for most brooch designs. Constructing these elements without soldering requires some thoughtful engineering. You'll want to feel comfortable with your cold-connecting skills before creating this brooch; the instructions are primarily geared toward forming the catch and joint.

Figure 1

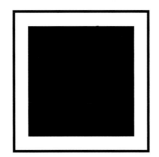

Figure 2

Figure 3

1. Design the brooch. Make the back piece out of one solid sheet of metal (see figure 1), and keep the top (figure 2) and back pieces very simple.

The positive and negative spaces in the middle piece (figure 3) are very important to the design. You must leave positive space in the middle layer to cover the negative spaces on the back layer formed from making the catch and joint. You may want to design your middle layer after completing steps 3 to 7. (When I designed my middle piece, I made a second frame that disappears under the top frame, creating the illusion that the middle piece floats under the top piece.) You can use more than three metal layers to create more depth to the brooch, if you wish.

WHAT YOU NEED

Sheet metal, 24 gauge

Scribe

Steel ruler

Saw frame and blades

Bastard file

Needle files

Flexible shaft

Flexible-shaft sanding accessories

Sandpaper, 400- and 220-grit

Chasing hammer and punch

Steel block

Assorted drill bits

Commercial pin stem with rivet

Flat-nose pliers

Round-nose pliers

Wire, 18 gauge

Flaring tool, if using tube rivets

2. Saw out the top piece, the middle piece, and the back piece. File, and then sand the pieces to a 400-grit finish. Determine the locations for the rivets. Dimple, and then drill the rivet holes on the top piece only (see photo).

BEFORE YOU BEGIN

The brooch is made in three layers: the **top piece** or frame; the **middle piece** or decorative layer; and the **back piece**, which has the catch and joint. Since you've already worked with riveting, planning space for rivets, and all the other basic techniques, I'll leave the design aspect and basic construction of this project up to you. The main focus of the directions that follow will be on creating the catch and joint.

3. Draw a straight line across the rear side of the back piece, about ¼ inch (6 mm) down from the top edge, as shown in the illustration. Always place the catch and joint above the centerline of a pin. If you were to place the catch and joint in the middle of the brooch, it would flop over.

4. Draw one line 1 mm above and one line 1 mm below the line drawn in step 3 (see illustration). This indicates the width of the foot and the width of the space between the flaps of the joint. Draw two vertical lines, each

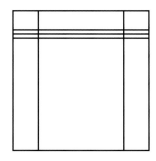

about 7 mm in from a side edge of the back piece, as shown. This line indicates the center of the catch and the center of the joint. (When you look at a brooch from the back, the catch is always on the left, and the joint is always on the right. This is because most people are right-handed.) Make sure the pin stem is long enough to fit this space. If it isn't, draw the vertical lines closer together. [My brooch is 1½ inches (3.8 cm) wide, and the pin stem is 1¼ inches (3.2 cm) long.]

5. Design the shape of the catch and joint. (Although mine is oval, it's much easier to make a square catch and joint, so I have written directions for this shape. Later, with practice, you can make fancier shapes,

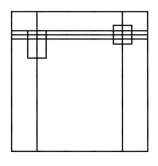

but for now stick to the square shape.) Measure the height of the connection on the commercial pin stem. Using this measurement as a guide, mark a square (approximately 5 x 5 mm*) both above and below the lines drawn in step 4 on the right side of the back of the pin (see illustration). Mark a 5 x 7-mm rectangle from the top line on the left side of the back of the pin as shown. Make sure these squares are centered correctly, using the vertical line drawn in step 4 as a guide.

*The sizes of the squares are approximate, depending on the commercial pin-stem connection and the size of bit available to drill the holes for piercing and sawing. Make smaller squares if your pin-stem connection is smaller than 3 mm. Make larger squares only if you have a larger drill bit.

6. At least 1 mm away from the squares created in step 5, mark a 4 x 7-mm rectangle for the foot as shown. Make the foot at least as tall as the commercial pin-stem connection, if not 1 mm taller. Remember that

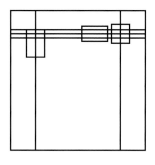

the drill hole made prior to sawing removes metal, so it's better to make the rectangle a bit longer.

7. Drill the holes for piercing and sawing out the shapes marked in steps 4, 5, and 6. Use the smallest drill bit possible that still allows room for the saw blade. (I used a .25-mm drill bit.) Drill the holes at

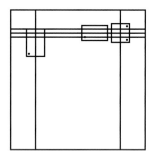

the points marked on the illustration as close to the marked lines as possible without drilling on them. Redraw a guideline to follow when sawing.

8. Pierce and saw out the front, middle, and back metal pieces. From the front side of the back piece, gently push up each sawn piece until you can grip the piece with the flat-nose pliers. The

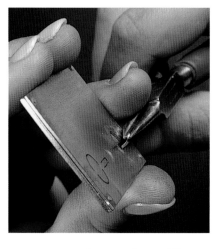

catch and the foot are easy to push up and grip. The joint is a little more difficult because you must keep the centerpiece stable. It's easy to break off the centerpiece here, so very gently push up the two sides of the joint. Curl the catch with the round-nose pliers, shaping it like an upside-down U rather than a sideways C (see photo, previous page, lower right). Leave room for the pin stem to easily enter the catch from underneath. The foot will be at an angle; you'll determine its exact height once you place the pin stem.

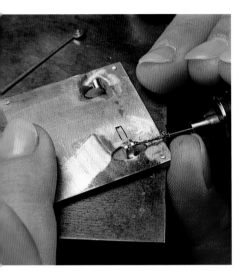

9. Dimple and drill the rivet holes in the pin-stem connection as shown. Open the joint enough to put the pin stem in place. The pin stem sits in the joint with its rounded side facing down as shown in the photo below. Use the pin stem rivets as a guide for making the ' drill holes on the joint. Mark the holes, and drill at a 90° angle to the sides of the joint. (I drill one side, then the other, and then drill through both at once to make sure they're even.) The drill hole should be the same size, if not slightly larger, than the rivets in the pin stem.

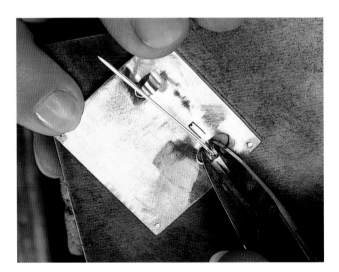

10. Put the pin stem in the joint. Use the flat-nose pliers to tightly squeeze the two joint sides together as shown. Once the pin stem is installed, adjust the height of the foot. The foot gives the pin stem spring in order

to secure it in the catch. Sand the ends of the catch, foot, and joint, so they won't snag on any clothing. Adjust the length of the pin stem as needed so it snugly fits into the catch without the sharp end protruding. If it's too long, snip the stem, and refile and sand the point.

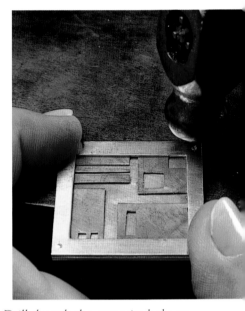

11. Measure the thickness of the three layers. Cut four rivets from the 18-gauge wire, each 2 mm longer than the thickness. Tightly hold together all three layers of the brooch with your fingers. Drill through one of the holes on the top sheet, and then the middle and back layers. Rivet the layers together at this point. Drill though the opposite hole on the top sheet, through the remaining two layers, and rivet (see photo). Drill and rivet the final two holes. Give the brooch a final finish.

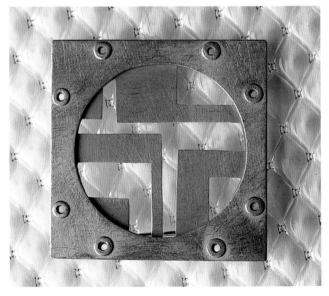

Alternate brooch design

E. Douglas Wunder.
Pendant with neck
ring, 2000. 3 x 2$\frac{1}{2}$ x
$\frac{1}{4}$ in. (7.6 x 6.4 x .6
cm). Silver, titanium;
constructed with cold
connections.
Photo by Larry Sanders

Abrasha. Earrings
with rivets, 2002.
$\frac{3}{4}$ in. (20 mm)
diameter. Stainless
steel, 18K gold,
diamonds; fabricated,
machined, cold
connected.
Photo by artist

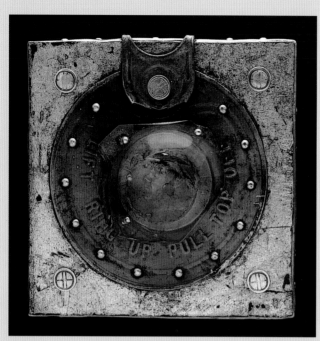

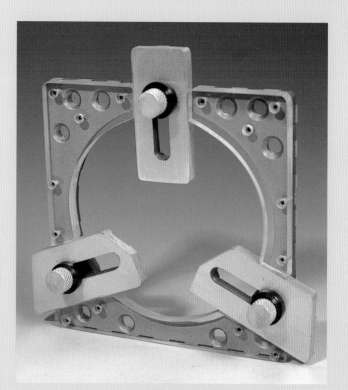

J. Fred Woell. *¿Como Esta? Pin*, 1997. 3$^{1}/_{2}$ x $^{1}/_{2}$ in. (8.9 x 1.3 cm). Wood, aluminum, brass, copper, glass, gold leaf; cold connected with 22-caliber shells, nails, epoxy. Photo by artist

Frankie Flood. *Slug or Slide Bracelet*, 2000. 4$^{1}/_{2}$ x 4$^{1}/_{2}$ x 1 in. (2.5 x 11.4 x 11.4 cm). Anodized aluminum, acrylic, stainless steel, rubber; cold connected. Photo by David Griffin

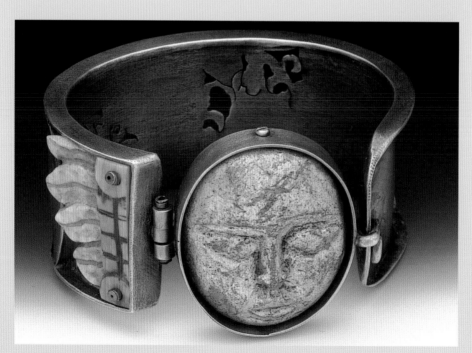

Eric Silva. Bracelet, 2000. 7 x 1$^{1}/_{2}$ in. (17.8 x 3.8 cm). Gold leaf, sterling silver, fossilized mammoth ivory, copper rivets; cold connected. Photo by George Post

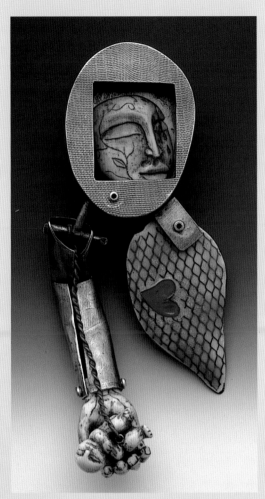

Eric Silva. Brooch, 2002. 4 x 2 in. (10.2 x 5 cm). Sterling silver, fossilized mammoth ivory, enamel, copper rivets; cold connected.
Photo by George Post

Thomas Mann. Collage button pin, 1997. 4³/4 x 2¹/2 in. (12.1 x 6.4 cm). Thermoplastic, antique postcards; cold connected. Photo by Will Crocker

Wesley Glebe. Rings, 2002. Titanium, 18K white gold, 24K gold, 18K rose gold, 24K gold rivets; cold connected. Photo by Michael A. Black

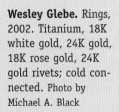

Amy Tavern. Necklace, 2001. 15 x ⁵/₈ in. (1.6 x 38.1 cm). Steel screen, sterling silver, beads; cold connected. Photo by Fred Miller

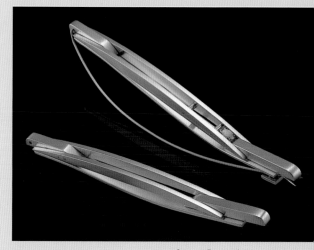

Matthew Feldman. Pins, 1999. 1³/₈ x 1⁷/₁₆ x ¹/₄ in. (3.5 x 3.6 x .6 cm). Sterling silver, 14K yellow gold, rose gold, handmade screws; tap and dye, press-fit, hand-cut, hand-fabricated, cold connected. Photo by Pam Perugi Marraccini

Elizabeth Garvin. Geometric pendants, 1997. Square and circle ¹/₂ x ¹/₂ x ¹/₄ in. (1.3 x 1.3 x .6 cm), oval 1¹/₂ x ³/₄ x ¹/₄ in. (1.3 x 1.9 x .6 cm). Sterling silver, peridot, amethyst, garnet; riveted construction. Photo by artist

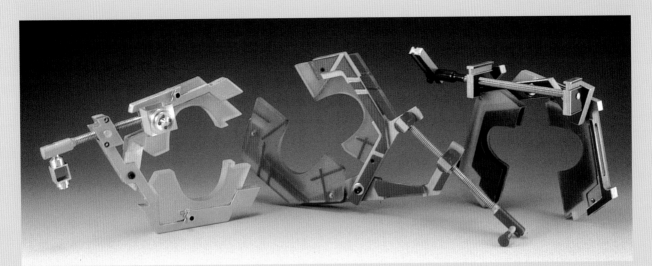

Frankie Flood. *1/4–20 Bracelet Series,* 2000. 4 x 6 x 2 in. (10.2 x 15.2 x 5 cm). Aluminum, acrylic, enamel, paint, stainless steel; cold connected. Photo by David Griffin

Debra Lynn Gold. *Shadow Play Earrings,* 2000. $2^2/5$ x $1^3/5$ x $^4/5$ in. (6 x 4 x 2 cm). Colored aluminum, sterling silver; pierced, fabricated, riveted. Photo by M. McKelvey

Boris Bally. *Diatom Brooches,* 2000. 7 x $1^5/8$ x $^1/2$ in. (17.8 x 4.1 x 1.3 cm). Recycled traffic signs, silver; hand-fabricated, hand-pierced, swaged, riveted. Photo by David Rubin

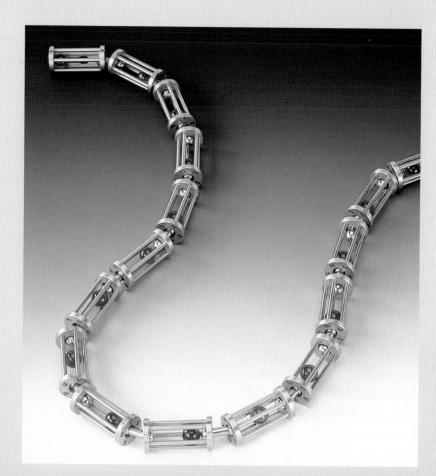

Abrasha. Ruby ball necklace with rods, 1998. ½ in. (12 mm) diameter x 19 in. (48.3 cm). 18K gold, stainless steel, synthetic ruby ball; fabricated, machined, cold connected.
Photo by Ronnie Tsai

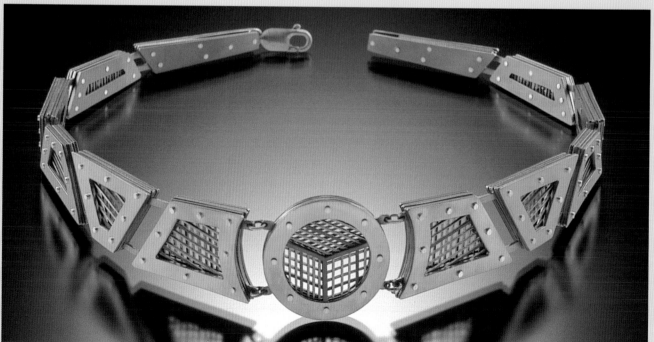

E. Douglas Wunder. Neck ring, 2001. 1 x 14 x ¼ in. (2.5 x 35.6 x .6 cm). 14K gold, titanium; constructed with cold connections.
Photo by Larry Sanders

Thomas Mann. Collage button pin, 1997. 4³/₄ x 2¹/₂ in. (12.1 x 6.4 cm). Thermoplastic, antique postcards; cold connected.
Photo by Will Crocker

Beth Piver. Rings, 2002. ³/₄ x ¹/₂ in. (1.9 x 1.3 cm). Silver, copper, bronze, brass, steel, assorted stones; riveted.
Photo by artist

Michele Nafalski. Bracelet, 2002. 1 x 8 in. (2.5 x 20.3 cm). Sterling silver, rubber rings; cold connected.
Photo by David W. Coulter

Debra Stoner. *Might Have Been a Coat Hanger...*, 1993. Steel wire, shaped plastic lenses, hex-head nuts; drilled, tapped, filed, cold connected. Photo by Paul Yonchek

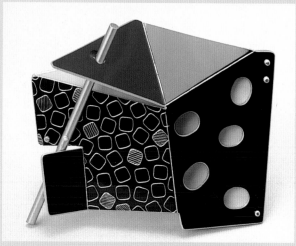

Debra Lynn Gold. *Home Repair Brooch*, 1998. 1⁴/₅ x 2¹/₅ x ⁴/₅ in. (4.5 x 5.5 x 2 cm). Colored aluminum, sterling silver; hand-engraved, pierced, fabricated, riveted. Photo by Sue Ann Kuhn-Smith

Abrasha. Computer hard disk brooch with bezel (front and back view), 1993. 2⁵/₈ in. (6.6 cm) diameter. Aluminum, 18K gold, 24K gold, sterling silver, stainless steel; fabricated, cold connected. Photo by artist

Elizabeth Garvin. Cube bracelet, 2000. ½ x ⅜ x 7¼ in. (1.3 x .9 x 18.4 cm). Sterling silver; hand-fabricated, drilled, connected with tube rivets and hand-formed flat wire links. Photo by artist

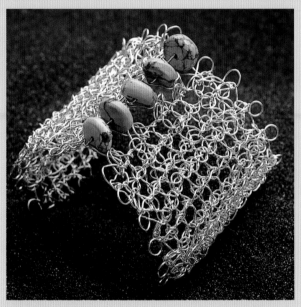

Michele Nafalski. Crocheted cuff, 2002. 2½ x 7½ in. (6.4 x 19.1 cm). Silver, turquoise buttons; crocheted. Photo by David W. Coulter

Matthew Feldman. Purse, 2001. French calfskin, Italian nubuck leather, sterling silver, 14K yellow gold, 14K white gold; hand-cut, hand-fabricated, drilled, tapped, cold connected. Photo by Clark Quin. Held in the collection of the Museum of Fine Art, Boston, Massachusetts.

J. Fred Woell. *Saint Elsewhere Pin,* 1986. 2¹/₄ x 2 x ³/₈ in. (5.7 x 5.1 x .9 cm). Wood, steel, copper, brass, gold leaf, 925; cold connected with rivets, epoxy. Photo by artist

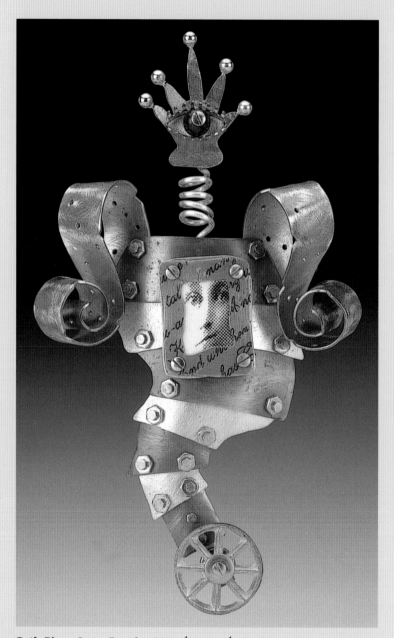

Beth Piver. *Jester Brooch,* 1999. 4¹/₂ x 3 x ¹/₂ in. (11.4 x7.6 x 1.3 cm). Silver, copper, brass, bronze, steel, computer-generated art, spinning and moving parts; cold connected, etched. Photo by Jerry Anthony Photography

Steve Midgett. *One Hundred Dollar Ring,* 1995. 1 x ³/₄ x ⁵/₁₆ in. (2.5 x 1.9 x .3 cm). Paper money, 18K gold; cold connected. Photo by artist

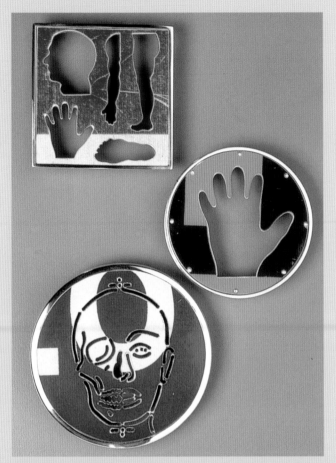

Debra Stoner. Untitled, 1996. Titanium wire, lenses; bent, cold connected with tubes. Photo by artist

Boris Bally. *Out of Hand, Corpus Rouge, Cranium Verde Pins* (Template Series), 1996. Largest: 3 x ¹/₂ in. (7.6 x 1.3 cm). Silver, recycled traffic signs; hand-fabricated, hand-pierced, riveted, swaged pin-backs. Photo by David Rubin

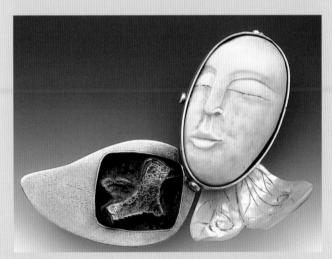

Eric Silva. Brooch, 2000. 3 x 2 in. (7.6 x 5 cm). Fossilized mammoth ivory, mother of pearl, sterling silver, bronze; hand fabricated, cold connected with rivets through the back side. Photo by George Post

Wesley Glebe. Rings, 2002. Titanium, 24K gold rivets; cold connected. Photo by Michael A. Black

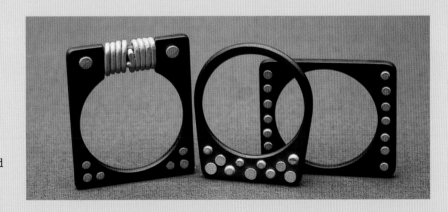

Acknowledgments

First, I must thank Terry Taylor for introducing me to Lark Books, for his creativity that urges me on, and for his all-around wonderful self.

I could not survive as an artist if it weren't for the invaluable discussions and support I've received from my artist friends: Caroline Manheimer, Kora Manheimer, Geoff Giles, and Steve Midgett. Many thanks.

My teachers—Tony Lent, Chie Teratani, Lori Talcott, Samuel Beizer, and Richard Barth (who taught me how to rivet!)—have inspired, informed, and encouraged me. I think of them every day.

I am thrilled to include the work of so many talented jewelers in the gallery pages. Thank you for sharing your images. Your amazing work with cold connections is a delight and an inspiration.

Thanks to my Ma and Pa, Maralee and Ron Gollberg, and my sister, Julie Bell, for believing that I can succeed in this business.

Lastly, thanks to the folks at Lark Books, who helped make this a fun and an easy job. Editor, Marthe Le Van rocks! Kathy Holmes, the art director, and Keith and Wendy Wright, the photographers, were amazing to work with. We made a great team, and I thank you guys so much.

Notes on Suppliers

Usually, the supplies you need for making the projects in Lark books can be found at your local craft supply store, discount mart, home improvement center, or retail shop relevant to the topic of the book. Occasionally, however, you may need to buy materials or tools from specialty suppliers. In order to provide you with the most up-to-date information, we have created a listing of suppliers on our Web site, which we update on a regular basis. Visit us at www.larkbooks.com, click on "Craft Supply Sources," and then click on the relevant topic. You will find numerous companies listed with their Web address and/or mailing address and phone number.

About the Gallery Artists

Abrasha
San Francisco, California
www.abrasha.com
Abrasha creates contemporary jewelry from unexpected combinations of precious and non-precious materials in forms well beyond traditional jewelry concepts. His work is exhibited in private collections, galleries, and museums, and is part of the permanent collection of the Smithsonian Institution's Renwick Gallery of the National Museum of American Art in Washington, D.C., and the Oakland Museum in Oakland, California.

Boris Bally
Providence, Rhode Island
www.borisbally.com
Boris Bally's work is permanently exhibited in museums and galleries in Europe and North America, including the Victoria and Albert Museum, the Smithsonian Institution's Renwick Gallery of the National Museum of American Art, Goldschmiedgesellschaft, and the American Craft Museum. His work has been featured in numerous publications and traveling exhibits. He is affiliated with The Society of North American Goldsmiths, The American Craft Council, and The Society of American Silversmiths, and shares his expertise in metalsmithing and jewelry design as an apprentice mentor at The Met School in Providence, Rhode Island.

Harriete Estel Berman
San Mateo, California
Harriete Estel Berman's new series of beads, fabricated from UPC bar codes, symbolizes a personal search for identity in a consumer-based society. Her work is represented by Sybaris Gallery, Mobilia Gallery, and Sienna Gallery, and is permanently exhibited in the Smithsonian Institution's Renwick Gallery of the National Museum of American Art, The Detroit Institute of Arts, The Jewish Museum, and Temple University's Tyler School of Art.

Matthew Feldman
Cambridge, Massachusetts
Matthew Feldman has translated his talent in design from working in leather to specializing in sculpting cold-connected metal jewelry. His work is exhibited in galleries, museums, and private collections across the United States and has been featured in *Ornament* magazine. Matthew has participated in numerous juried shows, served as a juror for The American Craft Council, and provided instruction as a guest lecturer for the Parsons School of Design and the Centre des Metiers du Cuir du Quebec.

Frankie Flood
Champaign, Illinois
Frankie Flood combines industrial and machining processes with contemporary jewelry design to create bracelets that are functional, aesthetically pleasing, and conceptually challenging. He is a member of The Society of North American Goldsmiths and exhibits his work in galleries across the United States.

Elizabeth Garvin
Elizabeth Garvin Design
New York, New York
www.elizabethgarvin.com
Elizabeth Garvin combines inspiration from architecture and industrial design with traditional jewelry-making methods to design forms, engineer movement, and develop new techniques for wearable art. Her work is exhibited internationally in galleries and museum stores as well as in home furnishing and design boutiques.

Geoffrey Giles
Candler, North Carolina
www.geoffreydgiles.com
Geoffrey Giles relies on hand-fabrication techniques with minimum tools to create fine metal jewelry that alludes to the impact of the industrial revolution upon human life and society. His jewelry was recently featured in "Transformations 3: Contemporary Jewelry and Small Metals" presented by the Elizabeth R. Raphael Founder's Prize at the Society for Contemporary Craft in Pittsburgh, Pennsylvania. His jewelry is available through Sienna Gallery in Lenox, Massachusetts.

Wesley Glebe
Wes & Gold
State College, Pennsylvania
www.wesandgold.com
Wes Glebe has been making jewelry in numerous and varied forms for most of his life. His current line focuses on the use of traditional joining methods, including riveting and wrapping. The inherent limitations in these techniques appeal to both the designer and engineer in his personality as he is forced to find solutions to design dilemmas. His work is available through galleries across the United States.

Debra Lynn Gold
Atlanta, Georgia
debralynngold@mindspring.com
Debra Lynn Gold holds an M.F.A. in Jewelry Design and Silversmithing from Indiana University and has shared her expertise as an instructor at Illinois State University, East Tennessee State University, Georgia State University, Arrowmont School of Arts and Crafts, and The Penland School of Crafts. Her work has been shown at the Smithsonian Institution's Renwick Gallery of the National Museum of American Art, The American Craft Museum, and at The White House. Public collections include the State of Georgia and the City of Atlanta. Debra's work is featured in books and professional journals and her work has received the Niche Award for Design Excellence.

Thomas Mann
Thomas Mann Design
New Orleans, Louisiana
www.thomasmann.com
Thomas Mann is a designer, jeweler, and sculptor who has experimented with collage and assemblage techniques to develop what is now his signature Techno-Romantic® style. His work has received numerous awards and is exhibited in private collections, galleries, and museums, including The American Craft Museum. Thomas' work has been featured in articles in numerous publications and is the subject of a new book, *Thomas Mann: Metal Artist*.

Steve Midgett
Franklin, North Carolina
www.mokume.com
Steve Midgett is an accomplished metalsmith and recipient of the JCK Rising Star Designer Award and Niche Award. In addition to the cold-connected jewelry he makes, Steve is internationally recognized as a leading authority on the mokume gane technique. He has authored instructional publications on this subject, taught workshops throughout the United States, and recently presented a lecture and workshop at Tokyo University of Art and Music in Japan.

Michele Nafalski
Hawthorne, New Jersey
Michele studied jewelry design at the Fashion Institute of Technology before obtaining a Bachelors of Metalwork from Montclair State University. She has been a regular participant of international jewelry symposiums in the Czech Republic and Poland, and has work in the permanent collection of the Granat jewelry company in Turnov, Czech Republic. She regularly sells her jewelry at fine art and craft shows in the New Jersey and New York area.

Beth Piver
Beth Piver Designs
Cumberland, Maryland
www.bethpiver.com
Beth Piver designs and creates a wide range of contemporary, mixed-metal jewelry with her husband Andy Vick. Her formal training in graphic design and computer graphics manifests itself throughout her work in bold shapes, striking juxtapositions, and computer-generated imagery. Her work is available in galleries and shops across the United States.

Eric Silva
Whittier, California
www.ericsilva.com
Eric enhances the organic contours and characteristics of natural materials, especially ivory, semi-precious stones, and rustic metals, with carving techniques and stains to create sculptural jewlery for wear or display. Each one-of-a-kind piece possesses a complex three-dimensional form with moveable parts constructed of rivets and hinges. Eric exhibits his sculptural jewelry at fine art and craft shows throughout the United States and on his website, www.ericsilva.com.

Deb Stoner
Portland, Oregon

Deb Stoner is a studio artist specializing in the design of handmade eyewear. She holds a Master's of Fine Arts from San Diego State University, and lectures and teaches at colleges and craft centers worldwide. She has designed eyewear for Anne Klein and Donna Karan, and curated the international traveling exhibition, "Op Art: Eyeglasses by Jewelers."

Amy Tavern
Seattle, Washington

Amy Tavern earned a BFA in Metal Design from the University of Washington with work that included a series entitled "Modern Chatelaines" and extensive research on jewelry and accessories worn at the waist. In 2001, she received a scholarship from the Women's Jewelry Association and the Culbertson Award to attend The Penland School of Crafts.

J. Fred Woell
Deer Isle, Maine

J. Fred Woell shares his extensive knowledge and award-winning design techniques as a teacher and lecturer at university art programs and workshops nationwide. His metalwork and sculpture has been presented nationally and internationally in prestigious exhibitions, such as "Objects: USA," "Good As Gold," "Poetry of the Physical," and "The Eloquent Object." His work is permanently exhibited in numerous public and private collections, including The American Craft Museum, the Smithsonian Institution's Renwick Gallery of the National Museum of American Art, The Detroit Institute of Art, and Museum Het Kruithuis, The Netherlands.

E. Douglas Wunder
Iowa City, Iowa
www.edouglaswunder.com

Douglas Wunder's inspiration for his layered and riveted jewelry comes from a combination of natural and technological objects. He is a regular participant in American Craft Council shows and he exhibits his work to sell at galleries and museum shops across the United States, including the Smithsonian Institution's Air and Space Museum Shop and The Los Angeles Craft and Folk Art Museum Shop.

Index of Gallery Artists

Index